Walking in the Vale of Clwyd
& Hiraethog

Approaching Pincyn Llys, Clocaenog Forest

Walking in the
Vale of Clwyd
& Hiraethog

Lorna Jenner

Alyn Books

First published in March 2000 by **Mara Books**, 22 Crosland Terrace, Helsby, Frodsham, Cheshire WA6 9LY.

Second edition published May 2009 by **Alyn Books,** The Nook, Pentre Road, Cilcain, Nr Mold, Flintshire CH7 5PD.

www.northerneyebooks.com
www.alynbooks.co.uk

ISBN 978 0 9559625 3 0

Front cover montage:

Carole Johnson, Lorna Jenner and Carl Rogers
Back cover photo: Carl Rogers

British Library Cataloguing-in-publication data.

A catalogue is available for this book from the British Library.

Whilst every effort has been made to ensure that the information in this book is correct, the author or the publisher can accept no responsibility for errors, loss or injury however caused.

Maps based upon out of copyright Ordnance Survey mapping

Printed and bound by Cromwell Press Group, Trowbridge, Wiltshire

Contents

Map showing the location of the walks

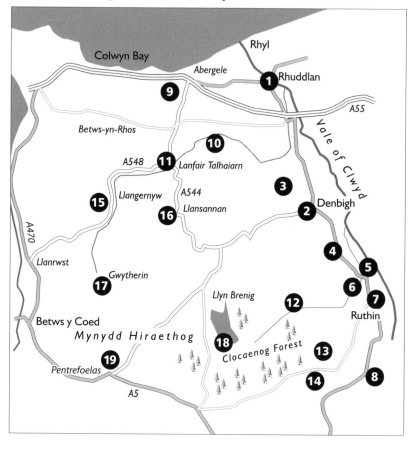

Introduction

THE VALE OF CLWYD and the adjoining moorland of Hiraethog have much to offer the walker—varied scenery and wildlife, historic towns, picturesque villages and a rich history. They are often overlooked in favour of the more rugged Snowdonian mountains to the west or the long Clwydian ridge to the east but they are well worth further exploration. If you want to escape the crowds who climb Moel Famau or flood into Snowdonia each weekend, discover the unspoilt and relatively uncharted countryside that lies between them. This collection of walks will help you to explore these less well known areas. Each part has its own special character.

The central focus of the Vale of Clwyd is the valley itself, threaded by contrasting rivers, the Clwyd and its tributaries, the Elwy and Clywedog. Their characters are shaped by the rocks beneath. The Elwy and Clywedog are fast flowing, particularly in the upper reaches, over rock and boulder clay and their levels rise rapidly after heavy rain. The Clwyd is more sluggish as it runs over porous rock. Its levels are slower to rise after rain and it carries sand and silt rather than gravel.

Moel Arthur from the Vale of Clwyd

Many of the walks have stretches of riverside walking but the contrasting characters of the rivers are best seen on the two walks that start from Rhewl. The Rhewl to Bontuchel walk follows the rocky Clywedog valley where the river tumbles over rocks between steep sided ravines whereas the Rhewl to Llanynys route is a flat riverside walk following the wide slower flowing Clwyd through cattle grazed meadows.

Viewed from the surrounding hills the Vale looks green and inviting. Lush meadows and pasture, edged with thick hedgerows, cover the wide valley floor. Sheep grazed fields, some divided by stone walls, dominate the lower slopes, interspersed with copses and areas of rolling parkland. Small farming hamlets, picturesque villages and historic market towns add to its special character. The spires and towers of churches stand out

in the Vale with battlements of ancient castles and forts on the higher ground. Much of the land was owned by a few large estates and many of the grand country houses built by these wealthy landowners still remain. Several walks lead through or alongside the grounds of these houses, the most impressive being Nantclwyd Hall at Llanelidan.

View from Clocaenog

Llyn Brenig

The Hiraethog moors probably look much the same nowadays as they did 5,000 years ago when the warm, wet weather after the last Ice Age allowed grasses, mosses and heathers to establish themselves. Ever since Stone Age man hunted on the moors over 8,000 years ago, mankind has been harnessing the resources of the moorland. From the Bronze Age, when farming techniques slowly developed, the moors have been used to graze livestock. By the 16th century cattle were regularly brought from the valley to the moors for summer grazing. The herdsmen lived on the moors with their stock, in simple one roomed stone shelters—hafods or hafotty—and some of these remain. In more recent times large areas have been flooded to form reservoirs, providing the only large stretches of open water in the area. The Aled reservoir was built in 1906, the long Alwen Reservoir was opened in 1921 and the largest, Llyn Brenig, in 1976. The Brenig walk follows the dam wall and has fine views of the moorland.

Another more recent development is large scale forestry. Agricultural opportunities are limited on the moors due to the peaty acidic soils but conifers grow well here and many parts are now heavily forested. The Clocaenog walk explores part of the forest and the dark greens of the conifer plantations are an integral part of the landscape on many of the walks.

The lower level walks often have magnificent views of the surrounding mountains. Most of the walks in the eastern vale have wide views of the Clwydian Range, those in the west around Gwytherin and Llanfair Talhaiarn have spectacular views of Snowdonia but there are also panoramic views on the Mynydd-y-Gaer, Llanddulas Quarry and Clocaenog walks.

The routes use footpaths and bridleways wherever possible but some rights of way in the quieter areas are rarely walked and, as a result, can be difficult to follow, so there are also many sections on quiet lanes. These often make a pleasant addition to the walk as many are edged with thick old hedgerows and grassy

Denbigh

banks dotted with wildflowers. The area is criss-crossed with old drovers' roads along which sheep and cattle were moved to market or between summer and winter grazing. Some are now shady sunken lanes, worn away by centuries of use, no longer used by stock and perfect for walking.

The unspoilt nature of the area is one of its greatest charms but there are often only limited facilities for the walker. Do not expect to find cosy teashops in the smaller villages that are far off the beaten track, and many of the characterful pubs only open in the evenings during the winter, so check before you set out or take flasks and provisions with you. The larger historic towns such as Denbigh and Ruthin, and many of the villages close to them, however, are well equipped for the visitor.

Most walks are enjoyable at all times of the year — the flush of spring flowers and newborn lambs; the meadows and moorland in summer, full of wildflowers and alive with birds and insects; rich autumnal colours and autumn mists in the valleys; the more open winter landscape with stunning views of snow covered mountains — all have their own qualities. A few of the walks, however, are best avoided at certain times of year. For example, the riverside south of Rhuddlan floods easily and should be avoided in wet weather and the moorland at Gwytherin can be extremely boggy and is difficult to navigate in the mist. The lower walks over farmland in the Vale can be unpleasant in damp conditions in June and July when the grass is long, before silage has been cut. Tastes and preferences vary and one person's idea of a gentle walk may be very different from another's but I have tried to give advice in the introductory walk description.

Please report any broken stiles or other route blockages to the rights of way department of the relevant county.

Conwy County Borough Council Public Rights of Way:
Tel. 01492 575460 publicrightsofway@conwy.gov.uk

Denbighshire County Council Public Rights of Way:
Tel: 01824706872 rightsofway@denbighshire.gov.uk

History

The area has a long and chequered history. Some of the earliest human remains in Britain have been found here. Neanderthal Man used the caves in the limestone cliffs over 200,000 years ago, probably camping at the cave mouths and fashioning simple stone tools for hunting the mammoths and bison on the plains below. Gradually, over thousands of years, the nomadic lifestyle of these early hunter-gatherers was replaced by a more settled agricultural way of life. Communities further developed when metal working skills were gradually introduced from Europe around 2,400 BC. Stone Age cairns and Iron Age barrows, used for burial, are dotted on the Denbigh Moors and the limestone outcrops suggesting that, as the climate improved, the communities began to use the higher ground, as the flat valley bottom was too marshy. By the Iron Age some larger settlements had developed. The most obvious remains are of the defended hill forts—a series of ditches and banks—visible on hilltops throughout the area.

The Roman invasion included Wales but most of their military action was along the coast and the Conwy Valley. There were relatively few Roman settlements in the Vale or on the moors, although the Roman road linking the forts of Deva (Chester) and Segontium (Caernarfon) passed through the sites of Rhuallt and St Asaph, en-route to Tal-y-Cafn in the Conwy Valley.

Moel y Gaer, an Iron Age hillfort overlooking the Vale on the western flanks of Moel Famau

Platform cairn near Llyn Brenig

After the Romans withdrew from Britain, the Saxons gradually took control of England but never succeeded in conquering Wales. They had a decisive victory against the Celts near Chester in 616 AD which effectively confined the Celts to the land that later became known as Wales, separating them from their kinsmen in Cornwall and northern England.

Conflict between the Saxons and the Welsh princes continued and for centuries the area was disputed borderland between England and Wales. In fact the old name for much of it, 'Berfeddwlad', means 'The Lands Between'. One result of the constant warring was the building of Offa's Dyke, a long earthen ditch and bank, built by King Offa of Mercia (now the Midlands), to define and protect his border with Wales.

Skirmishes between the Welsh and Saxons continued despite the Dyke as the agricultural richness of the Vale made it particularly attractive to raiding parties. The Saxons won control of the northern crossing of the Afon Clwyd near Rhuddlan in 796 AD although King Offa was reputedly killed in battle here soon afterwards.

Following the Norman victory at Hastings in 1066, the Normans were quick to take control of England, but, like the Saxons before them, they were unable to extend their influence much beyond Offa's Dyke. They were however, not content to leave the Welsh unconquered in the mountains on their western border. William the Conqueror subdued potential uprisings by giving lands along this frontier to his most powerful barons who were free to plunder the Welsh kingdoms and extend their own influence Once again the fertile Vale of Clwyd was an attractive prize to the northern baron based at Chester.

The Normans erected a series of castles to consolidate their positions, but it was not until the reign of Edward I in the 13th century that Wales was finally conquered.

The Welsh prince Llywelyn refused to swear allegiance to the newly crowned Edward and, in retaliation, Edward invaded North Wales and forced Llywelyn to surrender. In the agreement that followed Llywelyn forfeited most of his lands leaving him with just the highlands of Snowdonia, whereas his unscrupulous brother Dafydd, who had fought on Edward's side, was rewarded with the lands between the Conwy and the Dee.However, peace did not last long as Dafydd soon resented the interference of English officials installed by Edward at Denbigh. The two brothers united in rebellion. They had some success at first taking the castles at Hawarden, Ruthin and Hope, but Edward's armies finally crushed them.

Llywelyn was killed at Builth Wells in Mid Wales leaving Dafydd to fight on alone but he was eventually caught and died a horrific traitor's death, being hung drawn and quartered at Shrewsbury. The heads of both brothers were displayed at the Tower of London and the Welsh were subdued for a period.

Denbigh Castle

St Peter's Church, Ruthin

St Digain's church, Llangernyw

Edward rebuilt several Welsh fortresses in stone and commissioned others, developing a ring of stone castles in North Wales as a formidable show of strength—those at Rhuddlan and Denbigh are still imposing landmarks.

However peace was relatively short lived and the area continued to be caught up in the struggles between the Welsh princes and the English rulers. The most powerful uprising was led by Owain Glyndwr, who declared himself 'Prince of Wales' in 1400 and began his rebellion by sacking Ruthin in retaliation for the seizing of some of his lands by its tyrannical English lord, Henry De Grey. Glyndwr enjoyed almost a decade of success in his struggle with the English crown but he eventually lost support and died in obscurity. He remains, however, one of Wales' greatest folk heros.

It was not until the late 15th century that the politics stabilized and peace and prosperity followed. It was during this period that many fine and lavishly endowed churches were built in the Vale

Llanfair Talhaiarn

of Clwyd. Many are double-naved and have beautifully carved wooden ceilings. The large churches at Denbigh and Ruthin are outstanding, but several of the smaller village churches have their own special charm. One of the finest is that at Llanrhaeadr, famed for its stained glass 'Jesse window' and that at Derwen with its intricately carved rood screen and medieval preaching cross in the churchyard.

But during the Civil War in the 17th century, the area was again at the forefront of action. Denbigh Castle was the last unconquered Royalist stronghold in Britain. Charles I took refuge there in 1643 after his defeat at Chester and there are many stories of skirmishes between Roundhead and Royalist troops in the surrounding area.

These stormy events have been much written about but the area's cultural richness should not be overlooked. It has long been a centre for Welsh culture producing numerous nationally renowned bards and Welsh is still widely spoken, particularly in

Hiraethog. Bishop Morgan, bishop of St Asaph from 1601-1604, played a vital part in giving Wales its own Bible. His translation was instrumental in helping to preserve the Welsh language as he used a pure classical Welsh that helped establish a uniform standard which other writers then followed. Twm o'r Nant, an 18th century playwright renowned as the 'Welsh Shakespeare', spent his later years in Denbigh and performed his plays locally. Llanfair Talhaiarn was also a literary centre. John Jones, a 19th century poet who took the name 'Talhaiarn' when he was made a bard at the 1836 Bala Eistedffordd, was born there. Many of his poems have been set to music and some are still sung today. The Harp pub where he lived became the favoured meeting place for local scholars and writers. Llansannan's monument celebrating the five poets that lived there, the Henry Jones museum at Llangernyw celebrating the life of this illustrious Welsh scholar and the plaque at Gwytherin commemorating the local man who became the first Archdruid, all bear testament to the cultural richness of these Welsh communities.

English writers and artists were also drawn to the area. Beatrix Potter frequently stayed at her uncle's house, Gwaynynog Hall, near Denbigh and may have based her garden sketches for *'Tales of the Flopsy Bunnies'* here. Gerald Manley Hopkins, the Victorian poet who spent time at St Buenos college, Trechmeirion, wrote extensively of the beauty of the Vale of Clwyd. This is perhaps best illustrated by these lines from his sonnet *'In the valley of the Elwy'*,

"Lovely the woods, waters, meadows, combes and vales,

All the air things wear that build this world of Wales."

Farming

The Vale of Clwyd has long been renowned for the richness of its soil. Travellers told of a land where "throw in a stick and grass will cover it overnight". Agriculture remains the main land use and, to this day, the rich grass is still prized. Arable farming was also important until the 20th century and each settlement had its own corn mill. Farming practices have changed and transport networks improved so there is no longer a reliance on locally grown produce. Modern intensive arable farming is highly mechanised and needs large fields. Fortunately for the landscape of the Vale, the small irregularly shaped fields threaded by a network of narrow lanes are not ideal for this large scale production so the the attractive patchwork pattern of its landscape remains largely unaltered. Cattle still languidly graze on the lush riverside pasture and sheep dot the higher slopes much as they have done for centuries. Nevertheless the style of farming has undoubtedly changed.

Even grass production, to provide winter feed for the livestock, has intensified. Hay meadows, dotted with wildflowers, are less common nowadays as silage has taken over. Silage—fermented grass—is a nutritious winter feed for cattle and has become more popular as it is less weather dependent and of a more consistent quality than hay. After cutting hay needs turning in the fields for

Sheep have gradually taken over as the main moorland grazing animal

Cattle near Llyn Brenig

five days to dry out before baling. Silage, however, only needs to wilt for one day before being bagged for fermentation or, for larger scale production, chopped and packed into silage pits. Hence it is far better suited to the unreliable Welsh weather! Also, farmers can get several cuts of silage from each field between May and October, which significantly increases production. Walkers during the summer months are bound to see the large round silage bales tightly wrapped in black polythene and silage pits, covered in polythene and weighted down with tyres. The distinctive sharp sweet smell of silage around farmyards will become all too familiar.

Conditions on the moorland were too harsh for winter grazing but herdsmen took cattle onto the moors to feed on the new growth in the summer months. Sheep have gradually taken over as the main moorland grazing animal as they are hardy and need less attention than cattle. Dairy farmers nowadays tend to graze their cattle on the lower pasture during the summer, and overwinter them indoors, fed with silage.

Wildlife

The gently rolling farmland and open moors give the main character of the area but overall the landscape is a more varied patchwork. There are limestone outcrops, fast flowing streams running through steep wooded valleys, ancient woodland, conifer plantations, reservoirs and a flat wide estuary.

The flora and fauna are equally rich and diverse. Wildflowers thrive on the poorer soils in the limestone areas which, in turn, attract colourful butterflies. The pockets of wet woodland are luxuriant with huge ferns and mosses and the drier copses are dotted with primroses and violets in early spring and later carpeted with bluebells.

The moorland too is full of life. The purple heather covered hillsides in August, are broken up with patches of bright yellow gorse on the drier areas. There are wet flushes recognisable by

A dipper

Buzzard

the red and green spongy sphagnum mosses, dark green rushes and the white seed heads of bog cotton.

Birdwatchers too will find plenty to see. On the open moors red grouse may 'explode' from the heather at your feet and you may be lucky enough to glimpse black grouse in clearings and at the edges of the conifer forests. In the summer the plaintive haunting call of the curlew echoes across the moors. They leave the coast in the spring to breed on the moors. Other summer visitors include the sprightly little wheatear, often seen perched on a stone or clod of earth and recognisable by its white rump and black tail.

One of the most commonly seen and certainly the most spectacular of the larger birds is the buzzard, circling and wheeling overhead, with its distinctive 'mewing' call. Wading birds and wildfowl gather on the estuary and reservoirs in the colder months; herons are often seen flying slowly overhead or standing in the shallow water looking for fish; perky dippers bob across the streams; and an assortment of tits, finches and other small birds twitter and flit between the hedgerows.

Acknowledgements

Many people helped me in the preparation of the original book and this second edition. Thanks to those who shared their expertise with me: Phil Ebrell for his architectural comments, Malcolm Thomas for his farming advice and to Barbara Owsianka from Conwy County Borough Council and Adrian Walls of Denbighshire County Council for their advice on routes. Thanks to Alan Roe, Carl Rogers, Huw Davies and Carole Johnson for the use of their landscape photographs and to Simon Booth and Nigel Fairclough for their bird photographs. Thanks also to Gwen Evans, Sarah Brennen, Bob Nash and Bob Rudham who accompanied me on walks and checked the routes.

The Translators' Memorial, St Asaph Cathedral

Glossary of Welsh names

Afon ....*river*
Allt ....*hillside*
Bach / Fach..............................*little*
Bont / Pont ....*bridge*
Bryn ....*hill, eminence*
Cae ....*field, enclosure*
Caer / Gaer ....*fort*
Canol ....*centre*
Capel ....*chapel*
Carreg ....*crag or stone*
Castell ....*castle*
Cefn ....*ridge*
Clwyd ....*gate*
Coch / Goch..............................*red*
Coed ....*wood*
Cors / Gors................*bog or swamp*
Craig / Graig ....*crag*
Croes / Groes...........................*cross*
Cwm ....*coombe*
Dinas ....*city, fortress*
Ddu / Du ....*black*
Dŵr ....*water*
Dyffryn ....*valley*
Eglwys ....*church*
Faes / Maes........................*meadow*
Fawr / Mawr...........................*large*
Felin ....*mill*
Ffordd ....*road*
Ffynnon ....*well or fountain*
Foel / Moel.......................*bare hill*
Garn ....*an eminence*
Glas ....*blue-green*
Glyn ....*deep valley*
Gwern / Wern ....*alder coppice*
Gwyn ....*white*

Hafod ....*summer dwelling*
Hen ....*old*
Isaf ....*lower*
Llan ....*church*
Llyn ....*lake*
Llys ....*hall or court*
Lôn ....*lane*
Maen ....*stone*
Môr ....*sea*
Mynach ....*monk*
Mynydd ....*mountain*
Newydd ....*new*
Ogof ....*cave*
Pant ....*hollow*
Parc ....*park*
Pen ....*head or point*
Pentre ....*village*
Pistyll ....*waterfall*
Plas ....*house*
Pwll ....*pool*
Rhos.....................................*moorland*
Rhyd ....*ford*
Sarn ....*causeway*
Tomen ....*mound*
Tref ....*town*
Twll ....*cavern*
Twr ....*tower*
Ty ....*house*
Tyddyn ....*farmstead*
Uchaf ....*upper*
Waun ....*moorland*
Wen ....*white*
Y, Yr ....*the*
Yn ....*in*
Ynys ....*island*

Rhuddlan

Distance: *8 km/5 miles or 5km/3 miles*

A fascinating walk exploring the historic parts of Rhuddlan and the wide Afon Clwyd. The return route includes a stretch along a quiet road before following the old town ditch—a former Saxon boundary marker—to return to town.

NB - Some of the riverside sections of this walk can be impassable in wet weather. A shorter circular option is given but it is still worth walking down to the flooded meadows for the birdlife and views, providing you are wearing waterproof footwear (preferably wellies).

Start: There is a small car park in Parliament Street just opposite the Community Hall or roadside parking near the castle. *Grid ref: 024 782 (OS Explorer map 264).*

Rhuddlan was always of strategic importance, situated on a hill overlooking the wide floodplain of Afon Clwyd. The first settlement grew up beside a ford which was the most northerly crossing point of the Clwyd—whoever controlled the crossing point controlled the easiest invasion route to and from the heartland of North Wales.

For five centuries it was a site of conflict and a natural point for fortification. It was the site of a great battle between King Offa of Mercia and the Welsh. Later a Saxon fortified borough and a Welsh princely palace were built here.

After the Norman conquest it became a Norman stronghold. Edward I rebuilt both the town and castle in the 13th century, making it his administrative centre for the area. He even wanted to build a new cathedral there to replace St Asaph.

The walk

1. From the car park turn right and walk down Parliament Street to High Street. Turn left along High Street and then take the first right into Church Street to detour to St Mary's church.

The church was built in the 13th century as part of Edward I's new town. It is a typical low double-naved Vale of Clwyd church with a simple sturdy tower set in a lovely churchyard on a promontory above the river. The churchyard is packed with interesting tombstones and monuments—the 19th century Celtic cross to the Shipley family stands out and, at the back, a carved stone tribute to John Munt, a 19th century local sculptor.

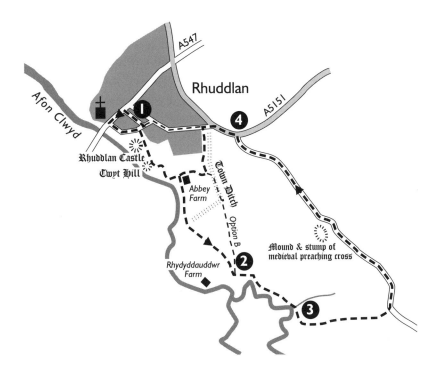

Return to High Street and detour right across the river on the footbridge alongside the old stone road bridge for a good view of the castle.

You can see that the river is straight from the castle to the sea. Edward I had this stretch of river dredged and straightened to ensure it remained navigable to his large warships and supply ships. A new quay was built and it became an important port, still in use until two centuries ago when the railways gradually made it redundant.

Look out for cormorants flying up and down or swimming on the water and diving down for fish.

Walk back up High Street and, beside Church Street, cross over into Castle Street. In front of the castle where the road bears left, continue ahead on a minor road, Hylas Lane. Just beyond the castle, where the road bears left, take the footpath on the right alongside the castle grounds, signed to St Asaph and Twyt Hill.

Edward I's castle at Rhuddlan

In 1277 Edward I commissioned the building of a new stone castle nearer the town, replacing the original wooden one at Twyt Hill. It was to become a key member of his ring of castles in North Wales built as a show of strength against the newly conquered Welsh. It was the first to be built on a pattern of three concentric rings of fortification, an innermost diamond-plan stronghold, surrounded by an outer circuit of lower turreted walls, with a deep moat linked to Afon Clwyd.

It last saw action during the Civil War when it was held by the Royalists. They finally surrendered to Parliament in 1646 and the castle was slighted in 1648 to prevent further miliary use. The castle is now owned by CADW and open to the public from May - October.

At the end of the track go through a kissing gate and continue ahead towards the mound, Twyt Hill. Bear left at a finger post on the path that skirts to the left of the hill—or detour up Twyt Hill for superb panoramic views.

Twyt Hill is the site of the first Norman fortress, a motte—an earth mound, probably crowned by a wooden lookout tower—built on top of the natural hill with a wooden bailey beside it that housed the troops. It was built in 1073, at the command of William the Conqueror, to consolidate the Norman advances in the area. It passed between English and Welsh until Edward I recaptured it in 1277.

Continue on the clear path, walking above but parallel to the river. Follow the path as it bears left away from the river, near a caravan park, to a road. Turn right along the road, passing Abbey Farm on the left.

This is the site of the 13th century Dominican friary, built within the Norman town. Earlier monastic orders tended to live in isolation from the world but the Dominicans built friaries close to towns and their friars preached to the local populations. The numerous medieval preaching crosses in churchyards throughout the Vale of Clwyd reflect this practice. Little now remains of the friary but bits of the original stonework are incorporated into the farm buildings. From the road, in a niche in the barn, you can see an effigy that must have once been in the friary.

Continue to a gate across the lane, where an old sunken path bears off to the right. Go through the gate ahead and follow the clear track across two fields. You can see farm buildings ahead on the right. At the end of a second field, where the track bends right towards the farm, continue ahead over a stile in the hedge. Walk across the field to another stile in the bottom left-hand corner.

Ahead are good views of the Clwydian Range, with Moel Famau, the highest point, clearly visible.

2. Climb the stile onto a sunken grassy track. Turn left away from the farm and walk along the grassy track to another stile. Cross the stile into a field and continue along the right-hand field edge down to the river. Cross a ditch and walk across the field keeping near the hedge on the left, with the meandering river on the right (NB—the path isn't clear, particularly when the grass is high in early summer). Continue ahead past where the field narrows and widens again, walking parallel to the left-hand fence. Cross an earth bridge (large pipe covered with earth) over the ditch and go over a stile beside a gate in the fence.

The fields beside the river flood easily and there is standing water throughout the year which attracts shelduck, the occasional cormorant and flocks of waders in the winter. During the summer many species of colourful damselflies and dragonflies can be seen near the water.

Dragonflies are larger and sturdier with wings outstretched at rest, whereas damselflies are smaller and more delicate with wings held upwards and together at rest. The dark winged, magnetic greenish-blue bodied damselflies are particularly eye-catching and common.

Bear half left across the next field to a ditch. NB—this ditch can sometimes be full of water and be difficult to cross. It was impassable when the route was rechecked in September 2008! An alternative shorter route (Option B) is given here to allow for all weather conditions.

You can see the squat tower of St Asaph cathedral ahead on the right. The cathedral has ancient origins. St Kentigern—a charismatic figure who later became patron saint of Glasgow—settled here in 560 AD with nearly 1,000 monks. When he returned to Scotland he consigned his Welsh monastery to his favourite pupil, a local man named Asaph. It is the smallest cathedral in England and Wales, and was destroyed time and again, situated as it was in the line of battle between the English and Welsh.

Option A (if the ditch is passable)

3. Bear left beyond the ditch and follow the fenceline partway along the edge of the next field to a stile marked Clwydian Way. Cross the stile and walk uphill away from the river, along the right-hand field edge. Cross another stile in the top right-hand corner and continue across the next fields in the same direction. When a farm comes into view ahead follow a fairly clear track across a field to the farm. Walk through the farmyard and follow the path to the road. Turn left along the road and walk for approximately 2.5km back towards Rhuddlan.

After 1km look for a mound on the left with a stone on top, just before a cluster of houses on the right. This is the base of a medieval preaching cross, perhaps used by the monks from the friary, when preaching to the local community.

4. At a T junction with the A5151, turn left and walk along the wide verge for a short distance. Turn left at the first junction onto Dyserth Road. Just before housing, turn left onto a signed path leading between a field and the backs of houses. Go through a small gate and continue along the path behind houses. Continue along this path, which becomes enclosed by two old hedgerows, crossing a stile partway along, until you reach a field.

This path formed part of the Saxon town defences and was originally a ditch, with a raised bank to the east. You can pick out the line of the old bank in places.

Turn right through a gate and follow the left-hand field edge towards caravans and farm buildings to reach the road beside Abbey Farm. Cross the road and take the footpath, signed to Twyt Hill and Rhuddlan Castle, and retrace your steps back to Rhuddlan. Opposite the castle turn right and then left past a tea shop into the upper end of Parliament Street, passing some picturesque cottages and an interesting chapel on the left.

Option B—if the ditch is impassable

Retrace your steps across the wet fields and walk up left-hand edge of next field to return to the sunken grassy track. Cross stile partway along on the right and then walk up the field, along the right-hand field edge. At the top of the field turn right along a wide grassy track between hedges. Cross a stile and continue across three fields, crossing two more stiles. At the far left-hand edge of the third field continue ahead along a wide grassy path between tall hedgerows.

This path formed part of the Saxon town defences and was originally a ditch, with a raised bank to the east. You can pick out the line of the old bank in places.

Cross a stile partway along and continue past the back of houses to join a road. Turn left along the road and walk back into Rhuddlan.

Turn left down Castle Street, opposite a fine old stone building that was the former Banqueting House. Just before the castle turn right alongside the Castle Tea Shop and follow this road back to the car park to complete the walk.

Rhuddlan Castle (walk 1)

Denbigh Castle and Moel Famau (walk 7)

Curlew breed on the moorland © Simon Booth

The woodland at Rhewl is carpeted in bluebells (walk 6)

The Ystrad Valley near Denbigh (walk 7) © *Carole Johnson*

Nantclwyd y Drae, Ruthin (walk 7)

Nantclwyd Hall (walk 8)

The limestone cliffs below Llanddulas Quarry (walk 9)

Rising out of the Clywedog valley near Cyffylliog (walk 12)

Looking into the Vale of Clwyd from the Clwydian Range

Moel Arthur from the Vale of Clwyd

Clocaenog Forest (walk 13)

Llyn Brenig (walk 18) © Carole Johnson

The mountains of Snowdonia seen from above Pentrefoelas (walk 19)

Denbigh

Distance: *7km/4½ miles*

The historic town of Denbigh with its ruined castle on the hilltop above the town, makes an ideal starting point for this walk. An exploration of the town, including an option to walk along the little visited medieval town walls, is followed by a peaceful walk through woodland at the base of the castle and along the picturesque Istrad valley.

NB—£5 deposit is required for the key to the walls. The key is available from the library (Telephone: 01745 816313 to check opening hours) and the castle custodian during the summer.

Start: There is parking in a small public car park on Vale Street or a larger one signed from Lenten Pool roundabout (£).
Grid ref: 052 661 (OS Explorer map 264).

Denbigh's strategic hilltop position made it an obvious site for fortification during the turbulent Middle Ages—its name actually means 'little fortress'. Encircling the hilltop castle are the medieval walls, which were built for additional protection. The medieval town developed within the confines of the walls alongside the castle. Despite the castle's commanding position, the steep gradient and shortage of water restricted the development of a market centre, so a new settlement gradually developed at the base of the hill. By the 16th century the walled town had been largely abandoned and the earliest of the civic buildings in the lower town date from this period. The town became an important centre for the leather industry between 16th and 19th centuries. It specialised in the manufacture of gloves but also provided leather for the many shoemakers in the town.

The focal point of the High Street is the 16th century Old Town Hall which housed the market beneath the colonnades on the ground floor and the court and administrative rooms above. Now the town library and museum, it is the starting point for the walk.

The walk

1. From the Library walk along the High Street on the left-hand side.

The High Street and the roads leading off it are edged with many fine period buildings — look upwards at the rooftops and upper storeys to fully appreciate them as the lower shop fronts often do no justice to the buildings. Some have elegant Georgian facades which occasionally cover older half-timbered frames. For example, The Crown, overtly a grand Georgian coaching inn with plastered facade and tall windows, is heavily beamed inside, showing its older origins.

Crown Square opposite the library, where the present market is held, is worth a detour — the imposing stone building facing the square is the present Town Hall. It used to house a market and was later used as a fire station — the tall windows and doors were large enough for fire engines to enter!

Turn left up the narrow alleyway of Broomhill Lane, beside the 'Old Vaults' pub. At the top of the lane bear right past terraced public gardens, edged with groups of cottages, and climb up to Burgess Gate.

Burgess Gate gave access to the medieval town and castle. The local Welsh were not permitted to pass through the gate into the upper area and were forbidden to purchase land within the walls, so they lived outside the walls

Walk through the gate and up St Hilary's Terrace to the green below the castle.

To the left is the tower of St Hilary's church, all that now remains of the chapel built to serve the castle and medieval town.

Turn right and follow the road up to the castle. It is now managed by CADW and there is an entry charge in summer to

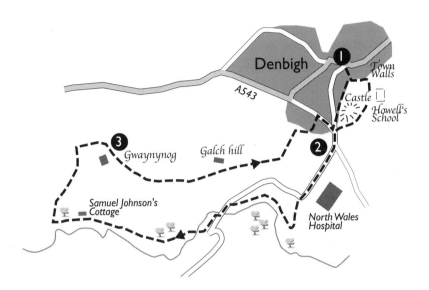

look round the interior, but you can wander freely around the outside.

This castle was once one of the strongest and largest in Wales. It was the chief stronghold of the Welsh Prince Dafydd ap Gruffydd until his defeat by Edward I in 1282. Edward commissioned the building of the stone castle, one of a chain of castles in North Wales that served to keep the defeated Welsh in check.

The commanding views from the green show what a formidable defensive position it occupied—it must have been almost impregnable!

The final military use for the castle was during the Civil War when Charles I sheltered there following a major defeat at Chester in 1646. Roundhead soldiers besieged the castle but the King had long escaped. The Royalists withstood the siege for 6 months but finally surrendered. The castle was dismantled in 1660 by the Roundheads and left to decay.

From the castle, walk back past St Hilary's tower and bear right along the lane leading down past the ruins of Lord Dudley's church below it.

Denbigh and its castle

Elizabeth I's favourite, Robert Dudley, held the lordship of Denbigh from 1563. A devout protestant, he began the church in 1578, intending it to replace the papist St Asaph cathedral as the centre of worship for the Vale. It was never finished—Dudley was very unpopular so money wasn't easily raised—but the lofty arches that remain give some idea of the scale and grandeur of his plans.

Just below Plas Castell, a group of Victorian Gothic buildings complete with battlements and tower, a small iron gate in the stonewall on the right gives access to the town walls. They are well worth a detour but please lock the gate when you leave and don't forget to return the key.

Following the ramparts above the town is a special experience from the moment you unlock the gate. Ferns and clumps of flowers grow between the stones, some sections are crumbling and the atmosphere is secluded and secretive. Firstly you are looking down to the gardens and rooftops of the town below. Further round there are wide views across the Vale, and you can imagine soldiers on sentry duty looking at a similar view many centuries ago.

From the walls turn right down road and, where the road bears left, take the footpath on the right below the walls. Walk downhill along the path for about 80m and, at a path junction, take the narrower tarmac path on the right running parallel with the walls. Pass the grand buildings of Howell's School on the left and continue on the same path skirting through woodland below the walls, with the fence on the left.

The steep rock faces on the right gave good natural defences to the walls and castle above.

Follow this woodland path to the road. Turn left along the road for about 100m, then bear right where the road forks, signed to Saron and Nantglyn.

The imposing building on the left was the North Wales Hospital, a Victorian mental hospital, built in grand Jacobean style (at time of writing the future of the building was uncertain and demolition was being considered).

2. Walk along the road for about 500m and where it bends right, take a signed footpath on the left, down a sandy track through woodland. Partway down the track turn right by a waymarker post onto a narrow stepped path. At a path T junction turn right onto a wider path that runs parallel to the river below and continue on this path. Just before a gate take a small path bearing left down the bank and over a stile into a field beside the river. Walk beside the river across the field. Continue on a grassy path through the next field passing a white cottage on the left. Cross a stile in the corner of the field, onto a road, beside a cottage drive.

Turn left along the road and, after about 90m, take a footpath signed on the right along the drive of a large house. (The drive is marked 'private' but it is a public footpath so walkers are entitled to use it. However, please respect the privacy of the owners as you walk through the grounds of their house!) Pass a vegetable plot on the right and the main house entrance on the left, then turn right between the vegetable plot and stable cottages and go through large wooden gates onto a track. Turn left along the track and follow the path uphill. Continue along the path with trees on the right and the river on the left.

The grassy clearings are rich in spring and summer wildflowers — clumps of tall purple foxgloves line the woodland edge and the meadows are gold with buttercups.

Ignore a footbridge and waymarker on the left and continue ahead on the same path over a stile next to a gate.

In the next field the small derelict and overgrown building on the right is the remains of Samuel Johnson's cottage. The 18th century writer who produced the first English dictionary, stayed here whilst visiting the Myddleton's of Gwaenynog. He was a renowned wit and moralist and is perhaps best known for some of his quotations such as, "It matters not how a man dies but how he lives" or "Marriage has many pains but celibacy has no pleasures."

At the end of this field where the path forks, turn right and walk diagonally uphill through woodland. Cross a stile into a field and follow the right-hand field edge with woodland on the right, climbing uphill to join a track. Bear right on this main track. Go through a gateway, ignoring a stile into the wood on the left. Bear left past a tiny quarry then cross the field to a gateway in the far corner. Go through gate and straight across a smaller field to a stone stile in the wall ahead. Continue a few metres ahead to a track leading from a farm on the left. Turn right through a gate and follow the track, skirting the old brick walls of Gwaenynog on the right. Just beyond the walls go through a gate/stile and follow the track past the entrance to Gwaenynog gardens to the main drive.

Gwaenynog Hall was once owned by the powerful Myddleton family — Sir Thomas Myddleton became Lord Mayor of London and bought Chirk Castle in 1595. Brother Hugh owned the Welsh silver mines and pioneered the provision of London's water supply. A later owner was Fred Burton whose niece, Beatrix Potter also stayed there. Her garden sketches for "Tales of the Flopsy Bunnies" were based on the walled garden which is sometimes open to the public.

3. Cross the main drive, ignoring the entrances on the right to the house and associated buildings, and continue ahead on the track through a gateway with good views of the Clwydians ahead. Go through a gate at the end of the first large field and head diagonally-left to a gate in the far corner of the next field. Walk along the left-hand edge of the next field. Cross a stile and continue downhill in the same direction with good views of Denbigh Castle on the left. Pass Galch Hill on the left.

This simple half-timbered house dates from the 16th century. It was owned by the Myddleton family and both Sir Thomas and brother Hugh were born there.

Climb a stile just past the house onto the lane. Ignore wooden stile opposite and turn right and walk down the lane for 50 metres to cross a stone stile on the left into a field. Walk diagonally-right across the field. Cross a stone stile into the next field and continue ahead, keeping the fence on the right, to a stile in front of houses. Turn right along a path behind houses. At the end of the path turn left onto the road through housing. Turn right at the end of this road and left at a T junction soon after, following signs to the castle. Turn right again past Castle Lodge. Where the road forks, either detour right up to the castle again or bear left down to the Burgess Gate to descend back to High Street to complete the walk.

NB—Please don't forget to return key to the town walls!

Henllan

Distance: *8 km/5 miles*

A pleasant walk centred on the attractive village of Henllan through rolling farmland and along old tracks.

NB—ome paths are prickly and overgrown in summer—shorts are not recommended!

Start: There is limited roadside parking in the village near the Llindir Inn, Henllan. *Grid ref: 024 681 (OS Explorer map 264).*

Henllan lies at the heart of the fertile Vale of Clwyd and this rich farmland brought prosperity. The parish was much larger then—over 16 miles long and 7 miles wide. The grand houses dotted in the countryside around the village were owned by landed gentry families. They had considerable influence and their large estates provided employment for most of the locals.

The thatched Llindir Inn is one of the oldest buildings in the village, dating from 1229. Its name comes from 'llin', the Welsh word for flax, grown in the fields behind. It is the only remaining one of six pubs in the village that served the once large agricultural community and the quarrymen from the nearby limestone quarries.

The walk

1. From the Llindir Inn, turn left and walk along the road out of the village, signed to Llansannan (don't take left fork). After approximately 200m turn right onto a clearly marked footpath. Follow the path above the river through woodland. (You may need to detour around a tree stump but do not wander into the

field). Keeping the river down on the left, cross a wooden fence
ahead and follow the path to the road.

*Ferns and mosses thrive in the damp woodland of willow and alder.
Beside the road is Henllan Mill, which was once driven by the fast
flowing river and ground corn from the surrounding farms before most
of the land was put to grass.*

Turn right and follow the road uphill back into the village
passing the church on the right.

*St Sadwrn's church has very early origins and this is reflected in
the village name—Henllan meaning 'old church', from 'hen'—old and
'llan'—church. It originated from the cell of the 6th century hermit, St
Sadwrn, but the present church dates from the 11th century. Its most
unusual feature is the separate bell tower perched on a rocky outcrop
above the sloping churchyard. This was perhaps because the bells,
summoning parishioners from the long parish to prayer, could be heard
better from the hilltop than from the church below.*

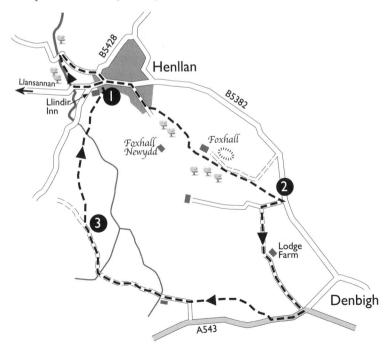

From the church continue along the road, signed to Trefnant, past the arch leading into playing fields. Take the first road on the right downhill, to rejoin the original road just above the Llindir Inn.

Turn left at the road junction and walk uphill, passing the Post Office on the right. Take the second lane on the right, just before the school, by a footpath sign. Continue to a farm drive then climb the stile to the left of the drive entrance and walk along the left-hand field edge alongside houses. Climb a stone stile ahead and follow a narrow woodland path (NB—May be quite overgrown!). Climb another stile and continue across the field alongside woodland with a fence, and later an old stone wall, on the right.

The Llindir Inn

The tall ivy clad ruin on the right, glimpsed through the trees and the old stone wall is Foxhall Newydd. It was begun in the early 17th century, by the Recorder of Denbigh, who wanted to build the largest mansion in the district but was never finished as he went bankrupt!

At the end of the field cross a stile beside the wall and turn left, walking alongside a fence, passing farm buildings and then the side of another old house, Foxhall.

Foxhall itself dates from medieval times, predating the nearby ruin of Foxhall Newydd, but it has been altered and added to many and so looks more recent.

Cross another stile beside the house (ignore path signed to the right) and continue ahead across a field.

The raised banks in this field are actually the remains of an Iron Age enclosure which was probably occupied as a farmstead.

Don't follow the drive ahead, but bear right across the field to a narrow path, crossing the remains of an old stonewall (waymarked) that leads into the woodland. Go through a gate (waymarked) and follow a narrow woodland track. (NB - This path may get overgrown!) Go through another gate and continue ahead on a path bearing right away from the golf course. Cross the stile into a field, and a second stile 100m ahead, then walk slightly left across the field towards farm buildings and the road.

There are now superb views of the Clwydian hills ahead.

2. When you reach the road turn sharp right by the side of the farm down a lane (not the main road). After approximately 200m turn left over a stile (may be overgrown) onto a grassy track between two hedgerows.

This was obviously once a route of more importance — probably an old drovers' path that once linked farms and may have lead to Denbigh.

Keep going downhill on the same path crossing a stile (NB - lower section may be very muddy as cattle obviously use it). Pass Lodge Farm buildings on the left and bear left over a stile, following the waymarker, past the farmhouse, keeping the hedge on the left. Partway along the field cross a stile in the hedge onto the drive to the house. Turn right along the drive and walk to the main road.

There are good views of Denbigh to the left.

Turn right along the road (take care—busy road!) and walk along the verge for about 200m to a layby. Turn right onto a footpath signed from the layby and walk diagonally-left across the field to a stile in the middle of the hedgerow. Then walk diagonally-right for a short distance across the next field to a stile beside a water trough. Cross a stile into a narrow field then turn immediate left and cross a stile in the adjacent hedge into another field. Continue straight ahead, across the middle of the field, heading towards farm (route should be clear through crops). Cross a footbridge over a small ditch and stile into another field and bear left and follow the fenceline to a stile in the top left corner. Continue in the same direction keeping a hedge on the left. At the end of the field turn left over a cattle grid and then, at a track junction, turn right onto a surfaced track. Follow the track past cottages. When the track bears right into fields, continue ahead along a grassy path—a sunken lane between two hedgerows.

This old track may have been an important drovers' route as the river has a ford marked on the map.

Follow this path downhill—it may be very overgrown in places—to a stream. Ignore a path to the left and cross the stream on the right-hand side to continue ahead on the same path. Ignore a second path signed to the left after about 250m and continue on the path as it climbs uphill for another 500m.

3. Turn right by a waymarker and climb steps and a stile out of the sunken lane into the field above. Walk along the fenceline ahead for a short distance then, approximately halfway along the field, walk diagonally-left to cross a hidden stile in the bottom left corner of the field. Cross a ditch then turn right and walk diagonally across the field to a gateway / stile halfway along the fence at the bottom of the field. Walk along the left edge of the next field towards Henllan—the church tower is a landmark on the hillside ahead. At the bottom of the field cross a footbridge over the stream.

The meadow beside the stream is full of plants that thrive in damp conditions—look for the dark green rushes and the pink flower spikes of ragged robin.

Bear slightly left up the next field. When you can see Henllan church ahead again, aim for a hedge / old wall in the middle of the field and walk with the hedge on the right to a stile hidden in the top corner of the field to the right of a corrugated shed. Walk along the drive of a private house to join the lane that leads back to the road by the Llindir Inn to complete the walk.

The village of Henllan

Llanrhaeadr

Distance: *8 km/5 miles*

The pretty village of Llanrhaeadr is an excellent starting point for an exploration of the gentle rolling countryside that surrounds it. It is typical of the Vale of Clwyd—green, sheep grazed fields edged with mature hedgerows, pockets of woodland and streams in wooded valleys, all set against the backdrop of the dramatic Clwydian ridge to the east.

Start: Some roadside parking is available in the village. Start at the church. *Grid ref: 082 634 (OS Explorer map 264).*

Llanrhaeadr means 'church of the waterfall' and it is these two features that give the village its special character. The 'waterfall' in question is now little more than a stream tumbling down from a spring in the hillside above the church. Legend has it, however, that St Dyfnog lived here in the 6th century and did penance under the waterfall. His virtues reputedly gave the waters healing powers and pilgrims travelled miles to bathe in these holy waters.

St Dyfnog's church itself is the focal point of the village. Built from local limestone, embellished with mellow buff and red sandstone, it is a handsome double naved church with a sturdy tower. A delightful cluster of old stone buildings huddle around the church—the old smithy which is now a pottery; the carefully restored smithy cottage beside it; the whitewashed almshouses edging the churchyard, bequeathed for the 'relief of eight poor persons of the parish' by the lady of the manor in 1729; and the 16th century inn opposite.

The church is most famous for its stained glass Jesse window, which casts a soft light into the church, but there is also much more to admire.

Gently curving sandstone arches separate and support the twin naves with their magnificent 15th century wooden carved ceilings. The section above the sanctuary is particularly special, each panel is intricately carved with a different design and below are vine leaves and carved angel busts.

During the Civil War Cromwell's soldiers kept watch for Royalists from the church tower during the siege of nearby Denbigh Castle. The soldiers were notorious for smashing windows with grave bones so the churchwardens dismantled the window and buried it in a dug out chest in the church grounds for safekeeping. It was later refitted and the huge chest that housed it now stands beneath the window.

The walk

1. After exploring the village and church, walk through the churchyard to the almshouses. Turn left through a small arch in the left-hand corner of churchyard. Cross the stream and turn right following a path uphill alongside the stream. Follow the path to a natural basin where the stream tumbles down the

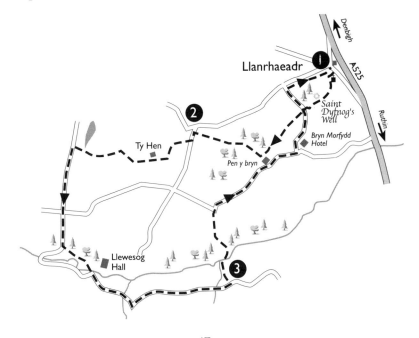

St Dyfnog's Well

fern-clad hillside into the stone bath below. This is St Dyfnog's Well.

It is incredible to find this carefully built deep stone bath, complete with steps in the midst of the woodland! Numerous slabs of dressed stone are dotted around the stream — remnants of the changing rooms and bathing areas built for the many visitors in its 17th and 18th century heyday.

From the well follow the path winding up the left-hand side of the hill. Go through a gap in the stone wall, turn right and walk along the path to a driveway. Turn left along the drive and then right into a field (clearly signed) opposite stone stables and a barn of the Vicarage. Diagonally cross the field to top left-hand corner. Cross a stile and follow the path up stone steps to the road. (NB This is the return path.) Turn left and almost immediately right onto another waymarked path across the golf course. Cross the first fairway heading for a waymarker post straight ahead, beyond the green.

Carefully cross another fairway, bearing slightly left and upwards to a waymarker alongside the wood on the right ahead, then walk along the fenceline with woodland on the right. About 50m before the black barn ahead, bear right on a narrow path along the fenceline to tee number 5, then climb over a stile into woodland on the right. Follow a narrow meandering path though woods to a track.

The woodland is carpeted with wildflowers in spring—bluebells, luxuriant spikes of early purple orchids and at the edges, masses of primroses.

Turn right along a broad forest track (left leads back to golf course). Take care to follow the yellow waymarkers through the wood as it is criss-crossed with tracks. Turn left at the next path junction along another woodland track, then turn right and follow the path to a stile at the woodland edge. Walk ahead across a field to a fence edging the top of a small industrial site. Continue walking, keeping the fenceline on the right, to a road.

2. Turn left along the road, then cross a stile into the second field on the right. Walk diagonally-left across the field to a stile in the far corner. Bear right in the next field, following the hedgerow upwards towards buildings in the far right-hand corner. Cross a stile onto a track and turn left and then right up the driveway of an old stone house, Ty Hen. Cross a stile on the right of the house into a field. Turn left and follow the field boundary for 30m alongside the garden (Do not miss stile and go into the old farmyard), crossing the stile and continuing straight ahead along the fenceline. Cross another stile into the next field. Turn right and follow the hedgerow along the right-hand side of the next two fields. At the next field junction, cross a stile to the other side of the hedge then turn left and continue in the same direction, gradually descending the hill. At the bottom cross a stile passing a small reservoir on the right (area may be boggy). Walk uphill along the field edge to the road.

Turn left onto the road and follow it downhill for approx 500m to a small crossroads. Continue straight across onto a quiet lane. Just after it becomes wooded on both sides, take the left-hand fork just before the main lane bends to the right. Follow this lane, running parallel to the river below, to buildings around Llewesog Hall. Follow the track past farm buildings then bear right in front of the house to cross a bridge to another lane. Turn left and follow the winding lane for approx 1.5km.

The huge conifers dotted in first field on the right indicate that this was once parkland associated with Llewesog Hall—the grand white Georgian mansion glimpsed through the trees on the left.

There are good views across the valley and Moel Famau soon becomes visible ahead. You may see lots of pheasants in the fields and along the lanes.

3. Ignore forestry tracks crossing the lane and continue uphill a short way to a signed footpath with gate on the left. Follow this path down an old sunken lane with tall hedgerows on either side. At the bottom cross a stream and, ignoring main track, bear right on narrow path uphill.

Charcoal burning was in progress by the stream at time of writing—look for the round metal charcoal pets in which the charcoal is made and stacks of wood.

Continue up the hillside on a small meandering path. At the top edge of woodland cross a stile and continue along an old track (NB - may be boggy). Go through a gate and then onto the road. Turn right along the road and continue for approx 1km.

Continue down the lane past Pen-y-Bryn on the left with the golf course on both sides. At a road junction turn left up a minor road with Bryn Morfydd Hotel down on the right. After approx 300m turn right onto the footpath used earlier to return to the village. Cross the field and turn left onto the drive of The Vicarage. Walk to the road and turn right. After a about 80m turn right onto a path running parallel to the road, beside an old brick wall. Continue to the end of the path, bringing you out by the almshouses above the churchyard, to complete the walk.

Rhewl to Llanynys

Distance: *7 km/4½ miles*

A flat, gentle circuit along two rivers with superb views of the Clwydian Range. It could be added to the contrasting Bontuchel route to make a long figure of eight walk—the Drover's Arms would be a good place to stop for lunch.

NB—An easy lowland walk but many stiles and it can be boggy in wet weather. There are also plenty of cattle and some of the herds may include bulls!

Start: Park in the car park by the recreation ground in Rhewl or on the roadside in the village centre.
Grid ref: 110 604 (OS Explorer map 264).

The walk

1. Walk back to the main road and turn right towards Denbigh. Just before the stone road bridge turn right onto a waymarked footpath into a field. Walk diagonally-left across the field to the river.

Cross a stile and follow an enclosed path behind paddocks and gardens, keeping the river on the left. Cross two small fields passing a small pond and the grounds of an old house on the right, then cross a small enclosure of young trees. Continue along the riverside for approximately 1km, crossing several stiles and ignoring a footbridge on the left.

Herons, with their long wings and distinctive slow wingbeats, are common. You may also hear the plaintive 'coor-li' call of curlews.

When you reach a larger stone bridge, go through a gate, then turn right and walk along the track from the bridge heading towards the Clwydian Range (ignore track on left partway along).

There are now wide views of the hills. Moel Famau, the highest point of the Clwydian Range, stands out, crowned by the remains of the Jubilee Tower that was built to commemorate 50 years of George III's reign. The original tall column blew down in a fierce storm just 52 years later. Its base was renovated in 1970 and was used to commemorate another royal jubilee when it was the site of one of the chain of beacons lit to celebrate Queen Elizabeth's silver jubilee in 1977.

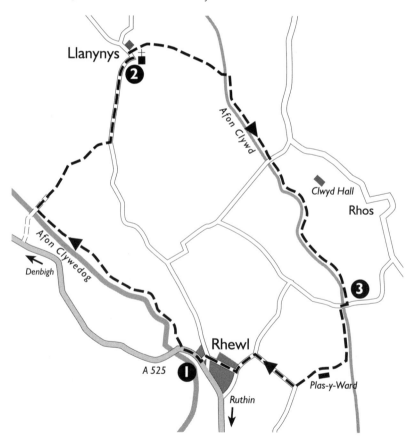

Follow the track along the field edge to a gateway in the right-hand corner of a field, at a junction of three small streams. Walk through a gateway over one stream and go straight across the next field to a gate at the far side. Cross the next small field, heading for a gate in the far left corner and cross onto a track. Turn right on the track and left onto the road. Walk along the road into Llanynys.

The views are magnificent now. Can you pick out the ramparts of the Celtic hillfort on Moel Arthur, to the left of Moel Famau?

2. Walk past the church and now closed pub then turn right onto a signed path beside the former pub.

The quiet hamlet of Llanynys, lying between the rivers Clwyd and Clywedog, is clustered around the simple stone church and ancient churchyard with its gnarled yews and tabletop tombs. Llanynys means 'church of the island' which suggests that the surrounding flat fields may once have been watery marsh.

The church was once very influential, the site of a 6th century monastery and the mother church of southern Dyffryn Clwyd. Its interior is large and spacious, befitting its former importance. Opposite the entrance is a large medieval wall painting of St Christopher, the patron saint of travellers, carrying the young Jesus across a river. He was often painted opposite church doorways so travellers could glimpse his image and be preserved from 'fainting or falling' all that day.

Walk down the path past a row of cottages on the left. Cross a stile into a small paddock / wood store. Cross this and then a second stile into a larger field. Cross this diagonally right until opposite the church, then continue straight ahead past two large trees in the middle of the field to a footbridge and stile in the opposite hedgerow (This field was planted with maize in August 2008 but path was passable). Cross the bridge and stile then bear diagonally right across next field to the hedgerow and follow the field boundary round as it curves left to a stile in the corner, by a cream house. (This field had been ploughed in August 2008 and was extremely muddy!)

Bellcote, Llanynys Church

Cross the stile and walk past the house to another stile. Walk along the left-hand edge of the next field then cross a stile onto a track where a drive joins from the left. Cross the bridge over the river, then climb right over the stile and immediately left over another stile. Turn right again to walk along the field edge with the river on the right below.

Dippers—small brown birds with white bibs—are commonly seen on the river, bobbing on stones or flying rapidly down the river. They walk underwater to feed on river insects, tadpoles and worms.

Continue along the riverside through fields, crossing stiles and walking parallel to the Clwydian Range. Cross a road and another stile and continue through another riverside field. Climb a ladder stile into the next field, passing the grand crenellated buildings of Clwyd Hall above on the left (NB: Beware - cattle and a bull are often in this field but they are fairly placid!). Cross a stile and continue through the next field, below a farm, passing farm buildings on the opposite bank.

There is a magnificent black poplar in the middle of this field, recognisable by its twisted bark and attractive in spring with its red tinged buds. The rounded hump of Foel Fenlli is visible behind it, crowned by a large hillfort.

3. Go over a ladder stile onto the road and turn right over the bridge, then left over a stile onto a riverside footpath on the opposite bank. Continue walking with river on the left.

Ahead are good views to Ruthin church and castle.

After passing a footbridge on the left turn immediately right along the hedgerow to a farm (Plas-y-Ward). Walk through the farmyard, past whitewashed farm buildings and a barn with stone arches on the right. Walk along the farm drive to the road. Turn right along the road and left at a T junction. Turn right just after the playing fields to return to the village and complete the walk.

Black poplar with the Clwydian Range behind

Rhewl to Bontuchel

Distance: *7 km/4½ miles*

This walk leads across fields and along the steep wooded hillside above Afon Clywedog, then returns along the rocky riverside into Rhewl. It is idyllic in late spring with bluebells and freshly opening leaves or in the dappled shade of summer. It is special too in the colder months when the river is in spate.

Start: Park in the car park by the recreation ground in Rhewl or on the roadside in the village centre.
Grid ref: 110 604 (OS Explorer map 264).

The walk

1. From the Drover's Arms pub turn right and walk along the main road over the old stone bridge. Cross the road just after the bridge opposite a small cottage. Take the clearly signed path along a metalled farm drive beside a cottage.

Continue uphill along the farm track through woodland. Ignore the woodland tracks on either side until you reach a clear fork in the main track which is signed with yellow arrows. Take the right fork and cross into a field. Continue walking on the clear path along the right-hand field edge beside woodland. At the far end of the field turn left in front of a corrugated barn and follow the right-hand fenceline to a stile in the hedgerow ahead. Continue ahead, gradually climbing uphill through fields, keeping the fenceline on your right and following the waymarkers towards woodland ahead.

There are superb views back to the Clwydians with mixed woodland clothing the valley sides.

Cross a stile into woodland and continue ahead, bearing slightly left, walking through tall conifer woodland along a clearly waymarked path.

The woodland floor is almost bare of vegetation here due to the lack of light penetrating through the foliage of the closely packed conifers—only occasional mosses and ferns where a pocket of light strays through. Compare this with the mass of greenery under the broadleaved trees further on—particularly rich in spring before the full tree canopy is out with bluebells, white stitchwort, and clusters of violets and primroses.

Continue along the woodland path into more open mixed woodland that skirts fields on the right. Continue straight ahead at a signed footpath junction, keeping the field edge to

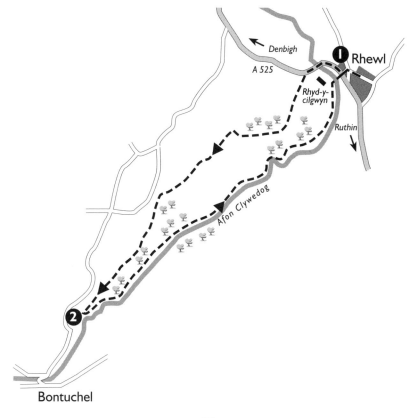

the right. Cross a stile into fields and continue straight ahead, with woodland in the valley on the left and farm buildings on the right. Cross a stile at the end of the field, back onto a narrow woodland path that skirts along the top of a steeply wooded valley, with fields to the right.

It is superb here in spring looking down the hillside when the wild cherry is in blossom with the dark greens of the conifers and paler greens of the freshly opening leaves of the deciduous trees. On the right before the path junction there is a dense carpet of bluebells beneath beech trees—a deep blue haze against the grey beech trunks.

Cross a stile into fields and continue ahead, with woodland in the valley on the left and farm buildings on the right. Cross a stile at the end of the field back onto a narrow woodland path that skirts along the top of a steeply wooded valley, with fields to the right.

2. Bear left down some steps to a path junction. Turn left and follow the woodland path as it gradually descends to the river. Continue beside the river all the way back to Rhewl (approximately 3km), ignoring two footbridges that cross the river.

In spring the smell of the white flowered wild garlic that tumbles down the river banks is almost overpowering. The river bed is much rockier than the slower flowing Afon Clwyd and is edged by rocky outcrops and crags. The rocks were lid down in a deep ocean 420 million years ago and fossils of sea creatures can occasionally be found. The rock isn't porous so water levels can rise quickly and, in the winter months, the river is a fast flowing torrent.

The Bagot family had a large estate, over 17,500 acres, here in the 18th and 19th century. This riverside path is known as 'Lady Bagot's Drive', as it was a favourite of hers and was once a scenic carriage route up to the Bagot's mansion at Pool Park.

Continue along the riverside path to a kissing gate. Go through the kissing gate and follow the track that leads between two cottages. Continue on the track as it bears right back to the riverside then continue walking along the riverside path.

You may notice a straight smaller stream running alongside the river and some old stonework chanelling it under the path—this may be a leat that drew off water to provide power in the past.

Continue straight ahead along the track, past the farm buildings of Rhyd-y-Cilgwyn farm, where the track becomes a surfaced road.

Amongst the modern barns and outbuildings are several much older timber framed buildings. The farm and Rhyd-y-Cilgwyn house itself, were also part of Lord Bagot's estate.

Bear right over the stone bridge and continue to the main road. Cross the road to return to Rhewl and complete the walk.

Looking towards the Clwydian Range

Ruthin

Distance: *10 km/6½ miles*

An exploration of this historic town and a pleasant circuit along the river and across farmland to picturesque Llanfair Dyffryn Clwyd. The walk back to the town is across fields and lanes with superb views of the Clwydian Range.

NB—It can be very wet walking crossing fields in June before the silage has been cut!

Start: There is plenty of parking in the car parks near the Craft Centre. *Grid ref: 125 585 (OS Explorer map 264).*

Ruthin has had a turbulent history—its name means 'red fortress', referring to its hilltop castle. In the Middle Ages the area was much disputed borderland between England and Wales. The Welsh and English inhabitants mixed little. The Welsh lived in Well (Welsh) Street and Mwrog Lane, whereas the English kept close to the castle for the protection it gave in Castle Street and Dog Lane.

The town saw conflict on several occasions, most dramatically when it was sacked by Owain Glyndwr in 1400, in his revolt against the tyrannical English Lord Grey of Ruthin. Most of the buildings were burned down and the town was completely rebuilt in the early 15th century. Many of these half-timbered medieval buildings still remain.

The walk

1. From the roundabout by the Craft Centre, walk up Market Street to St Peter's Square in the centre of the town.

The imposing stone building on the left towards the top of Market Street is the Town Hall and adjacent is the Market Hall which still houses regular markets. The livestock market is now held on the outskirts of the town.

Narrow winding streets, lined with tightly packed old buildings of assorted styles and materials, climb steeply up the hillside to St Peter's Square. The square itself is edged with a wonderful mix of buildings — half-timbered, brick, whitewashed and stone. Look upwards at the rooftops — wavy and uneven with old mellow tiles and slates and an array of windows. The elegant Georgian Castle Hotel dominates and, beside it, the Myddleton Arms with its three tiers of dormer windows, known as the 'eyes of Ruthin'.

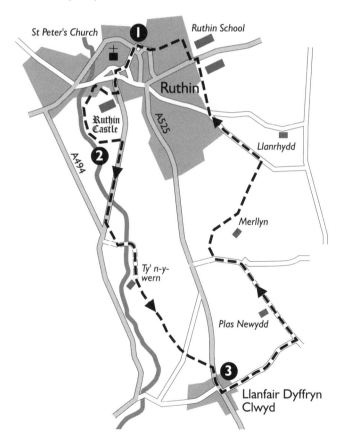

Ruthin square

One of oldest buildings, built in 1401, is now the National Westminster Bank. It used to house the Old Courthouse and had a gibbet where criminals were hanged on the north west wall!

This route through the town takes in some of the most attractive streets. (Alternatively, you may prefer to just wander at will around the town centre before picking up the walk by 'The Wine Vaults' on the corner of Castle Street and St Peter's Square.)

Walk to the Post Office at the opposite end of the square from the Nat West bank, behind which you can see the tall spire of St Peter's church. Enter the churchyard through tall wrought iron gates on the right of the Post Office.

This large church was founded in 14th century as a 'collegiate' church, staffed by a community of priests, who lived in the Old Cloisters that adjoin it. It stands out from other Vale of Clwyd churches as it is the only one with a spire, added during a Victorian restoration, which is a landmark for miles around (You can tell the spire is more recent as the stone is much more regularly sized and shaped.)

An attractive cluster of buildings edge the churchyard — the lofty cloisters with their pointed windows, the simple single storey almshouses and, at the back, the original grammar school buildings.

Return to the square and walk along the right-hand side. Take the first right down Clwyd Street, which is packed with period houses and shops.

Many of the buildings are medieval timber-framed refronted during the 18th and 19th centuries. Towards the bottom, opposite the Star Inn is the Town Gaol. The building edging Clwyd Street dates from 1775 when relatively few prisoners were held for long periods. The taller imposing Victorian building at the back was based on Pentonville and looks more secure and austere, complete with its small barred cell windows.

Walk back up the opposite side of Clwyd Street and bear right where the road forks up a narrow lane, Upper Clwyd Street, passing the 15th century Spread Eagle Bookshop on the right. At the junction with St Peter's Square turn right down Castle Street, with the colonnaded Wine Vaults on corner.

Castle Street too is packed with period houses. Most notable is the half-timbered Nantclwyd y dre on the right, one of the oldest townhouses in North Wales. It has recently been restored, with each room reflecting a different period in history, and is open to the public.

Ahead is the gatehouse to Ruthin Castle. The castle was begun in 1277 as part of Edward I's formidable ring of castles built as a show of strength after his capture of North Wales. It saw much action during the subsequent Welsh revolts but was last used for military purposes during the Civil War when it was a Royalist stronghold. The Roundheads laid waste to the castle after the Royalist defeat in 1646. The present house was built within the confines of the medieval castle in 1826 in Victorian Gothic style and was for many years a grand private house, whose owners entertained fashionable Victorian and Edwardian Society. It is now run as a hotel.

Just before the castle gatehouse, turn right under an arch and follow a narrow path between stonewalls, known as Cunning Green. Follow the path through a second arch. Then bear left and follow a paved path alongside the castle walls.

There are good views of the gaol, watchtower and rooftops of Ruthin from here.

At the end of the path turn right and then immediately left. Then turn left again through a gate into Cae Ddol, the playing fields. Continue ahead, keeping the castle walls on your left and the river on the right—you may hear the calls of the castle peacocks! Pass through a small kissing gate and continue alongside the fence until you reach a stone bridge across the river.

The river is clean and full of life. Small white flowers of water crowfoot float on the surface during the early summer and you may see dippers—small brown birds with white bibs, bobbing up and down on rocks in the river. The bridge is a good viewing place.

2. Go through the small tunnel under the bridge. Go through a kissing gate then turn left and walk along the left-hand side of the field. Cross a stile onto the road. Carefully cross the road and turn right to walk along the pavement beside the road for about 800m, ignoring a lane on the left. Just before a road on the right, take the signed footpath on the left through a gate and immediate right through a second gate.

Walk diagonally-left across the field, heading for the far left corner. Cross stile and onto a drive. Turn left along the drive, and follow it to the farm. (NB Do not be surprised to see bulls in the surrounding fields as this farm specialises in them!) Just before the farmyard go through the second of two gates on the left into a field. Turn right and walk parallel to the barn across the field to a gate in the hedgerow ahead, just to the left of a large willow. Go through the gate and walk across the next field to a gate in the opposite fence. Beyond a gate follow a track uphill towards farm buildings, passing a raised bank on the left.

The raised bank is the remains of a moated medieval homestead which

The 'Eyes of Ruthin'

was presumably replaced by Ffynnogion farm, the farmhouse ahead on the left, which dates from the 16th century.

Instead of bearing left to the farm buildings, keep walking straight ahead with the hedge on the right, to a stile in the corner of the field. Go straight across a small field and cross a stile into the next field. Continue across the next field to cross a stile beside a water trough (very muddy!), then walk diagonally-left across the next field to a ladder stile beside a large white house. Cross a very narrow field to the road.

This white house was formerly Eyarth station on the Corwen-Ruthin-Denbigh railway line and the narrow field is where the line used to run.

Turn right along the road and then left almost immediately through a small kissing gate onto a footpath along the left-hand field edge. Keep going in the same direction across two fields to the road. Turn right and walk along the road into Llanfair Dyffryn Clwyd.

65

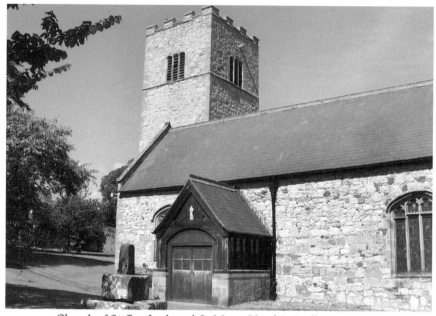

Church of St Cynfarch and St Mary, Llanfair Dyffryn Clwyd

The village centre is particularly attractive with its stone almshouses, village school and White Horse pub set around the fine 15th century church. There are wide views of the southern Clwydian Range from the back of the churchyard.

3. Pass the pub and turn left into the churchyard and then, after exploring the church, leave through a small lych gate beside the churchwarden's house. Walk along the lane to the road and turn left along the road. Follow this road for just over 1km. Where the road bears sharply right turn left onto a farm track (signed footpath) beside a lodge house.

17th century Plas Newydd is just visible through the trees in its grounds on the left. The row of limes edging the track and the dotted parkland trees in the surrounding fields suggest that its formal grounds once extended further. There are superb views of the Clwydian Range to the right.

Follow the track, passing the entrance Plas Newydd Farm

on the left, and continuing along the track to the road. Turn left onto the road and after 250m, take a signed footpath on the right, beside the drive to 'Merllyn'. Walk along the right-hand field edge. Part way along the field, just after a gate on the right, cross a stile in the hedgerow and then walk along the right-hand side of that field, now walking towards the hills.

Continue to the end of the field, then cross a stile in the hedgerow just beyond. Continue walking towards the hills along the next field edge. Cross another stile and walk across the middle of the field, to a gate in the hedge opposite (now walking towards Moel Famau, the highest hill in the Clwydian Range) then continue along the left-hand edge of fields to the road.

Turn left along the road and continue for about 750m. Just after a road joins from the right turn right up steps onto a concrete path alongside playing fields. Continue along this path past the Leisure Centre and Bryn Hyfryd School and continue to the road. Carefully cross the road and walk down the main drive of Ruthin School opposite.

The Grammar School was originally in the churchyard of Ruthin church but was moved to these grand purpose-built buildings in 1891. When prisoners escaped from the town gaol, boys from Ruthin School were occasionally used to help run them down! It is now a private school.

Beyond the school bear left and walk downhill along a private road edged with houses. At the end of the road cross Greenfield Road and walk down to the roundabout by Tesco. Cross the roundabout to return to the Craft Centre car park and complete the walk.

Llanelidan

Distance: *8km/5 miles*

A delightful circuit from this picturesque village through parkland and across wooded hills.

NB — Some sections through the woodland may be quite overgrown in summer and can be muddy — trousers and boots are recommended!

Start: Park on the road in Llanelidan or by the village hall. *Grid ref: 109 505 (OS Explorer map 264).*

Llanelidan's 15th century church with its pretty double bellcote, village hall, handsome stone pub and cricket green form an attractive group, standing amidst fields, whilst the main housing is on a nearby lane.

The walk

1. From the village hall turn left and walk along the road passing the church and pub. In about 40 metres, and immediately after the road crosses a stream, turn right onto a signed footpath alongside the stream. Walk past the cricket pavilion and bear half-left away from the stream across the field to a stile in the middle of a wooden fence. Cross the stile and continue ahead to another smaller stream—aiming for the stump of a felled oak in the hedge. Cross the stream by a large stone slab to the right of the stump, then bear right and climb diagonally up the field to a footpath waymarker and a stile onto the road. Turn right and walk along road for around 400 metres to an attractive cluster of old farm buildings on the right. Don't turn right onto the signed right of way down the driveway, but cross a stile to the left of the drive entrance, following a waymarked footpath through trees and into a field.

Walk ahead towards a clump of pines on a hillock, with the farmhouse on the right. Walk to the left of the hillock then downhill towards a lake, making for a stile in the far corner of the field by weeping willows at the far end of the lake. Cross the stile onto the road.

The lake and the surrounding wetland attract waterfowl, particularly in winter — black and white tufted duck and Canada geese are common.

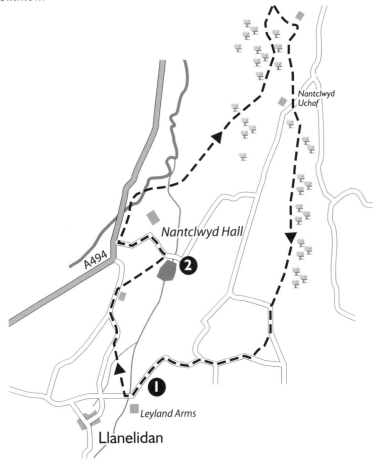

2. Turn left and walk along the lane to the main road.

The grand country house over the hedge to the right is Nantclwyd Hall. The gardens have been elaborately restored, and feature stone gazebos, ornamental bridges and sculptures.

At the main road (A494) turn right and walk along a broad grassy verge for roughly 400 metres. Just beyond a stone bridge on the right and opposite the lane to 'Clocaenog', turn right onto a signed footpath through the hedge. This crosses the course of the old road and goes into the woodland ahead. Walk through the woodland for about 60 metres, bearing left on a narrow path that leads onto the manicured lawns of Nantclwyd Hall. Walk ahead with the river on the right, crossing the drive to the house (which passes over an ornate bridge on the right) and continue ahead to a large gate in the fence.

Nantclwyd Hall

There are superb views of the mansion as you look down the driveway. The oldest part dates from the seventeenth century but it was extended and altered in the eighteenth and nineteenth centuries. In the 1950s and '60s it was elaborately remodelled by Sir Clough Williams-Ellis, the architect famous for the design of Porthmeirion.

Go through the gate or climb the wooden bars in the fence beside it and walk along the riverside to a pretty wooden footbridge. Cross the footbridge and walk diagonally-left across open grassland.

There are more good views to the right of the mansion with the lake in front. Colourful dragonflies and more slender-bodied damselflies dart across the edges or rest in the vegetation at the lake edge in summer.

Continue to a small concrete bridge over a stream. Cross the bridge then climb diagonally-left across parkland. Walk uphill through dotted trees between a large fenced copse on the left and the main woodland on the hilltop to the right.

Continue contouring along the hillside parallel to the wood on the right. Pass a second smaller fenced copse on the left. At the far corner of the copse, turn right and walk to a gate and stile leading into the woodland.

Follow a narrow path leading half-left uphill through the trees.

The strong smell of wild garlic, with its dark green leaves and white flowers, fills the woodland in early spring, and is followed by a carpet of bluebells in May.

At the top of the wood go through a gate into a field and go ahead along a track to a large gate. Go through the gate into the next field and keep ahead until the Clwydian Range comes into view along with farm buildings ahead. Turn left and walk across the field to another wood—there is no longer a fence across the field but two large boundary trees roughly show the way.

There are good views of the Clwydian hills on the right as you walk across the field.

Go through the gate into woods and follow the footpath ahead

Ornamental bridge at Nantclwyd Hall

(can sometimes be a bit overgrown in summer). This soon bears left through the woodland. Continue on the path to the woodland edge beside two ruined cottages. Cross a stile in the fence ahead beside a corrugated iron barn, then walk straight ahead for 75-100 metres or so to the end of the high hedge on the right. Turn right here along a rutted and sometimes muddy farm track that swings rightwards back towards the woods. The track weaves between scrubby bushes and becomes better established to eventually run alongside a stone wall with woodland on the right. Continue downhill to a gate and stile with a cottage on the left. Cross the stile and bear right along a track.

Walk along the track for about 500 metres eventually, leaving the woods. Cross a stile next to gate into a field on the right and walk diagonally-left across the field to a stile leading into a lane. Turn right along the lane for about 50 metres then, just before the drive to a house on the right ('Nant Clwyd Uchaf'), cross a stile on the left into a field and walk ahead along the right-hand field edge, with woodland on the right.

Part way down the field, cross a stile on the right into woodland. Follow a path directly through the woodland for about 50 metres to a gate leading into a field on the far side. Go through the gate and follow the left-hand field edge, keeping woodland on the left. Cross two large fields separated by a stile.

In the corner of the second field cross a stile under trees and cut directly across the following field, just to the left of centre, to a stile in the far corner. Turn left immediately over another stile into woodland and follow the path to the right, continuing in the same direction as before along the woodland edge. The path is difficult to find in places and may get overgrown in summer.

Wildflowers flourish on this grassy limestone bank at the woodland edge. In spring cowslips abound; look also for the spikes of early purple orchids.

Stay close to the woodland edge with fields to the right. Count the fields to your right. At the far fence of the second field bear right past the fence corner and then go ahead through trees to find a stile in the fence ahead beneath high hawthorn bushes. This takes you back into fields. Walk ahead along the field edge with thinning woodland on the left. Continue in the same direction, going through an old gateway in the hedge. Continue across the next field with the hedgerow on the right to a stile leading into the lane.

Turn right along the lane and at a T junction in a few metres turn left. Walk up the lane until you come to a pretty stone chapel on the left at the top of the rise. Just opposite the cottage attached to the chapel turn right and cross a stile into the field. Bear left across the field down to a stile in the hedgerow below. Turn right and walk down the road for 1km / ¾ mile back to Llanelidan to complete the walk.

Llysfaen &
Llanddulas Quarry

Distance: *6.5km/4 miles or 8km/5 miles*

A refreshing walk, climbing the limestone hill above Llysfaen, walking through pasture and leafy woodland on the lower slopes with dramatic cliffs and panoramic sea views from the hilltop. NB—The section leading up to the quarry is steep.

Start: Park in the lower part of Llysfaen, beside the bus stop, toilets and playground, at the junction of Tan-y-Craig Road and Dolwen Road.
Grid ref: 893 767 (OS Outdoor Leisure 17 & Explorer 264).

The walk

1. Walk past the playground and turn left up Dolwen Road, passing a chapel on the right and then bearing right along the road. 100m beyond the chapel, turn right along a drive in front of houses, signed "North Wales Path" (NWP). Continue along this drive, with fields on the right. A few metres past the drive to 'Bryn Celyn' on the left, turn left over a stile into a field, signed NWP. Walk across the top of grassy fields, with a stone wall on the left, contouring along the hillside.

To the right are wide views of the rolling Vale of Clwyd—a farmed patchwork landscape with irregularly shaped fields, edged with thick hedgerows and pockets of woodland.

At the end of the wall, ignore a stile onto a track on the left and continue ahead, walking parallel to the track. Pass a caravan site on the left behind a stone wall. Pass a stile and waymarker, and bear slightly left, still contouring round the hillside, following the direction of the waymarker. Pass a breezeblock building on the right, and continue on a grassy path past rubble. (This section is a bit difficult to follow but keep looking for NWP waymarkers and skirt around a caravan park.) Continue contouring along the hillside, with a fence on the left, crossing another field boundary with a stile and waymarker.

Continue in the same direction until you reach a stile in the fence on the left. Cross the stile and turn right onto a track that contours round the hillside. Where the path bears right downhill cross a ladder stile on the left into a field. Continue straight ahead along a grassy track. Where the track dips, a few metres ahead, walk diagonally-left uphill to a stone wall. Turn right and walk with the stone wall on the left continuing to follow the wall where it curves left up the hill to a fence and waymarked stile. (The path may not be very clear in summer but the wall is a useful marker.) Cross the stile and bear right uphill along a narrow path, following the direction of the arrow, onto the open hillside.

Wildflowers thrive on the poor thin soils above the limestone bedrock. Wild thyme, with its pink flowers and small scented leaves, delicate

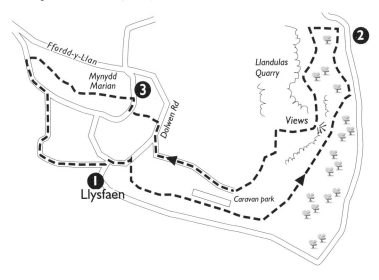

Looking out to sea from the limestone cliffs below Llanddulas Quarry

blue harebells, and ladies bedstraw, a small creeping plant with clusters of tiny yellow flowers, are all common in the summer. There are also patches of more acidic soil on which purple flowered bell heather and bracken flourish.

The variety of flowers provide food and shelter for many insects. You may notice the papery cocoons of the burnet moth in the summer. This distinctive red and black moth is one of the few day flying moths and is frequently seen on the rough grassland around the quarry. A variety of colourful butterflies thrive also—delicate blues, browns and coppery oranges—and, if you look carefully, you may also notice grasshoppers camouflaged in the grass.

Cross a ladder stile over a stone wall and follow the waymarker straight ahead across grassland. (NB - It may not be very clear in summer when the bracken and grass are high.) Do not go left along the path that leads up to the high limestone crag but continue ahead on narrow path (through bracken in summer) that skirts along the base of the crag. Follow the path for approximately 500m to a gate. Go through the gate and continue along the path down the hillside, heading towards the coast. The path leads through woodland, with occasional rocky outcrops. Ignore a footpath crossroads and continue on the same path until you come to a T junction of paths. Turn sharp left uphill here, leaving the North Wales Path.

2. Follow this broad track as it gradually winds up hill. At a path T junction, just below the quarry fence, turn left and follow a narrow track. Walk along the path for approximately 1km, with the fenced-off quarry above on the right (you cannot see much but you can often hear it!) and woodland on the left, gradually climbing to the top of the hill. After a short steep section, go through a kissing gate and onto the hilltop.

There are superb panoramic views from the hilltop: the coast with the Great Orme protruding out to sea to the west, with the working quarry in the foreground; Snowdonia to the southwest; Llanddulas and the sea to the north; wooded hills edge the valley to the east with the Clwydian Range on the skyline in the distance and the lush Vale of Clwyd unfolds to the south. The line of rubble that was once a rampart on Pen-y-cordynn-mawr hillfort on hillside to the east is clearly visible.

From the hilltop, walk back to the quarry fence and follow it around the quarry to the left (west). Turn left alongside the first hedgerow, walking away from the quarry (may be overgrown and prickly in summer!). Climb the ladder stile in the bottom right-hand corner of the field onto a grassy path, between two fields. Follow this track as it bears left and then runs between two stone walls, until you reach a farmyard.

Go through a gate and walk past farm buildings along the farm drive to the road. Turn right along the road and continue for approximately 750m to a T junction, opposite a pretty chapel, attached to Holly Cottage. To return to the start in Llysfaen turn left down the road.

For a longer walk turn right and walk uphill along the road. Just before a pebble-dashed house go left through a metal kissing gate into a football field and walk along the right-hand field edge.

Go through another kissing gate then bear left across next field, following direction of the arrow. Cross a stile in the far corner of the field and follow an enclosed path to a lane. Where the lane meets a road turn right past houses on the right. Just after the last house turn left onto a signed path onto Mynydd Marian.

Mynydd Marian was designated as a Local Nature Reserve in 2001 due to the wealth of plants and animals that thrive on the limestone. Clumps of early purple orchids and, later, common spotted orchids flower in the early summer and many species of butterflies fly throughout the summer and are particularly noticeable during warm, still spells.

Follow the broad stony path uphill towards a house. Bear left onto a narrower grassy path partway up and follow this path uphill passing the stone house on the right.

The stone house, Telegraph House, was built in 1841 by the Trustees of Liverpool Docks as a signalling station. It was one of twelve stations built along the North Wales Coast to send messages and reports of ships between Holyhead and Liverpool. The first messages were sent by semaphore but this was later replaced by telegraph. The record for sending a semaphore message from Liverpool to Holyhead and receiving a reply in Liverpool was 53 seconds!!

Continue ahead on the path onto the summit, passing an informative panel on the left. Follow the broad grassy path ahead as it gradually descends. Go past some large stone boulders by a Mynydd Marian sign and turn left onto a track and follow this left past houses down to the road.

Turn left along the road and, after about 120m, bear right onto a narrow road, Geulan Rd, and follow this steeply downhill (Partway down the hill, where the road bends right, a signed footpath left offers a shorter route across fields back to Llysfaen but this route was unclear when checked in Feb 2009) Continue uphill on the road, turning sharply left (road now called Bwlch-y-Gwynt). Continue along road for another 500m past housing, keeping ahead where a road joins from the right, back to the start of the walk in Llysfaen.

Mynydd-y-Gaer & Llanefydd

Distance: *8km/5 miles*

A refreshing walk over Mynydd-y-Gaer—site of an Iron Age hillfort—through woodland in the valley and then contouring around the base of the hill back to Llanefydd.

NB—There are some steep sections up Mynydd-y-Gaer.

Start: Park in the public car park in the middle of Llannefydd beside the church and village hall and on the opposite side of the road to the 'Hawk and Buckle Inn'.
Grid ref: 982 706 (OS Explorer map 264).

Llanefydd is a sleepy little village set amongst gently rolling farmland. Its focal point is the fine double-naved church with the whitewashed old inn opposite.

The walk

1. From the car park turn left and walk along the lane out of the village, towards Llanfair Talhaiarn, passing the school on the right. Opposite a lane joining from the left, go through a gate into a field on the right. Walk along the left-hand edge of the field then follow far hedge to gate in bottom right corner, with Plas Heaton farm ahead. Go through the gate and turn left to walk along the left-hand field edge to the next hedge, heading towards Mynydd-y-Gaer. Go through a gate, partway along the hedge, then continue uphill along the left-hand edge of the next field. Climb a high stile in the top left corner and continue uphill across a small field, towards a wooden fence. Go through gate on left into a small enclosure then through a second gate onto the road beside a house.

Turn left and walk down the road until it bends sharply left. Turn sharp right up a lane beside a 'no through road' sign. Turn left onto a signed grassy track immediately past Bron Hwylfa cottage. Follow the track uphill, bearing slightly right at a path fork onto a narrow grassy path. Go through a small gate onto the open gorse-covered hillside. Follow a narrow grassy path through the gorse, bearing left along the hillside.

The top of Mynydd-y-Gaer is wide and open, with panoramic views — Snowdonia to the west; rolling pasture and tree-clad hills with small reservoirs in the foreground to the south; the Clwydians to the

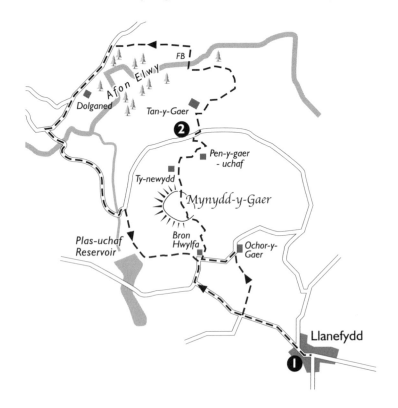

Plas-uchaf Reservoir

east and the sea to the north. The ditch and bank which still, in part, surrounds the summit, are the remains of an Iron Age hillfort. The commanding views and steep sided slopes must have made it an ideal defensive site.

In summer the gorse is full of activity—the small birds flitting around with dark backs and paler orangish underparts may be whinchats and stonechats. Their habitat gives the whinchat its name as 'whin' is an old name for gorse. Listen for a sound like two pebbles being banged together which is the distinctive call of the stonechat.

When you can see a fence on the right and reservoirs below on the left, turn right on a narrow grassy path through the gorse towards the summit of Mynydd-y-Gaer. A modern cairn, in the field to the right of the path, marks the highest point.

From the high ground follow the broad grassy path between two fences leading over to the northern side, Descend the hill, joining a track coming from the right by a cattle grid, and continue downhill, passing a cottage on left.

Where the track splits, take the less clearly defined path to the right, walking with gorse and grass on the left and an old stonewall on the right. At a gate and telegraph pole bear left on the grassy path, keeping the stonewall on the right. Where the main path turns right at the corner of the wall, continue ahead and down onto a very narrow path that bears right through the gorse (can be overgrown and hard to see). Follow this path as it zigzags down the hillside through the bracken to the lane below (heading for the clearly visible footpath sign beside the lane).

2. Turn right on the lane and go through a gate. After a few metres turn left down a farm drive (Tan-y-Gaer). Just before the farm turn sharp right down an old track between two hedges. At the bottom of the track where it enters a field, turn right along another track.

Follow this track for over 500m as it gradually descends the hillside (NB—can be very muddy). At the bottom of the hill go through a gate into a field and turn left across the field to a small gate in the far left corner, leading into woodland. Walk along the woodland path with the river on the right. (NB - the path is narrow and uneven in places.)

Follow the woodland path to a footbridge on the right. Cross the footbridge and walk across a field towards a white house. Turn left into grassy woodland just before the gate of the driveway. Then walk parallel to the river along a very narrow grassy path that may be overgrown with nettles and thistles in summer. Continue in the same direction, keeping the fence on the right-hand side, to a gate. Cross stile to left of gate and follow the clear path diagonally uphill then cross stile into field. Cross next field to a gate in the opposite hedge. Go through the gate and walk steeply uphill to another gate in the top left corner of the field. Follow the left-hand fenceline and, at the top of the field, cross a stile on the left into woodland and then turn immediately right to reach the road.

Turn left onto road and walk downhill for about 500m. Soon after passing the drive of Dolganed farm on the left, bear left at

Afon Elwy west of Mynydd-y-Gaer

fork onto a small lane. At the next road junction turn left and follow this lane for about 300m, over the river (Afon Elwy) and past a caravan park. Continue on lane for another 750m, climbing steeply at first and later descending again, turning sharp left into a hollow then uphill again to a gate. Go through the gate and turn right onto a grassy path that contours round the base of Mynydd-y-Gaer.

Follow this peaceful track, passing a small reservoir on the right. Beyond the reservoir, go through a small gate and continue ahead on clear path along the woodland edge, ignoring a second gate on right and a path to the left into the woodland. When the path eventually meets a road junction (the lane leading up Mynydd-y-Gaer is ahead), turn right and walk downhill along the road to another junction. Turn left and, where this road meets a more major road, turn left again and walk along the road for approximately 1km back into Llannefydd to complete the walk.

Llanfair Talhaiarn

Distance: *8km/5 miles*

A refreshing walk from picturesque Llanfair Talhaiarn, leading along the peaceful Nant Barrog valley, then contouring around Moel Unben with superb views of the Snowdonian peaks, returning to the village along a peaceful lane.

Start: There is plenty of parking in a car park beside the bridge leading into the village from the A548.
Grid ref: 927 702 (OS Explorer map 264).

The walk

1. From the car park exit beside the toilets, turn right along the main road into the village, past the Black Lion pub, into the square. Walk through the square. Just past the Post Office turn right along a tarmac path, leading uphill. After a few metres the path forks but continue ahead uphill to a road beside the church.

The church, set on the hillside in a particularly pretty churchyard, is well worth a visit. The monuments inside demonstrate how much village life was dominated by one family, the Wynnes, who owned nearby Garthewin Hall from the 17th century. The most lavish are those of the family themselves but some of the simpler tablets on the north side of the church are in memory of valued servants. In the churchyard there are gravestones erected for a gamekeeper and another for the Garthewin coachman.

To the right of the church drive, under the old yew tree is a granite obelisk which marks the grave of John Jones, a local 19th century poet who was made a bard at the 1836 Bala Eisteddfod and took the name

'Talhaiarn' after that. Many of his poems have been set to music and some are still sung today. He was born in the adjacent house, Hafod Y Gan, which was then 'The Harp Inn', and became a meeting place for scholars and poets. A few metres further along the road is the village school with its unusual octagonal bell turret.

Turn right past the church, then immediately left onto a lane running steeply uphill. Follow this lane out of the village, passing

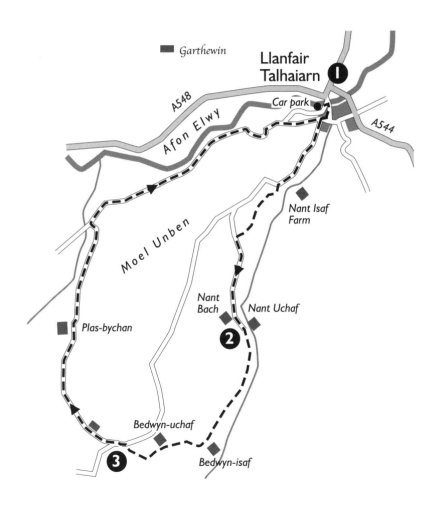

a farm drive with footpath sign on the left. About 100m further up, just beyond farm buildings on the right, turn left at another footpath sign through a gate into the field. Follow the hedgerow along the left-hand side of the field, with Nant Isaf farm down in the valley below on the left. Keep walking alongside the hedgerow to a metal stile in the fenceline ahead. Cross a stile and continue ahead to a white house. Skirt around the field edge above the house, crossing the drive, and continue to cross a stile in the hedgerow. Continue ahead across the field to another stile then follow the left-hand fenceline across the next field to a stile onto the lane.

Turn left onto the lane and continue downhill for approximately 600m, passing Nant Bach farm on the right and Nant Uchaf on the left at the bottom of the hill.

2. Go through a gate and continue along the lane, little more than a track now, with a stream down on the left. At a track junction bear right on a rising grassy path along the hillside, ignoring the left fork that leads down to a farm. Go through a gate and continue ahead on the track until you reach the farmyard of an old derelict farmhouse.

Go through the gate into the farmyard, then turn right immediately through a gate and walk along the side of the house. Turn left and walk behind farm buildings, going through another gate. Continue ahead for approximately 50m beyond the buildings then go through another gate into a field.

Walk across the field beside the hedge towards farm buildings visible ahead. Partway across the field cross through a gate to the right-hand side of the hedge and continue walking along this field edge, passing barns and a farmyard on the left. Continue along the field edge until it joins a farm drive, then walk up the drive as it bears right. Part way up the drive, turn left through a gate and walk across the next field to a farm ahead. Pass the farmhouse on the right and go through two gates onto the farm drive. Follow this for approximately 300m, down to the road.

3. Turn left and walk downhill on the road. Where the road bends left, take the track on the right, beside a small building, signed to 'Ty-newydd-foel'.

There are superb views of the Snowdonian mountains on the left as you walk along this path—Moel Siabod stands apart on the left, then the Snowdon group, the jagged Glyderau and the more rounded Carneddau. The foreground of gentle green hills, broken by thick hedgrows and stone walls snaking up and down the valleys, is a pleasing contrast to this rugged backdrop.

Keep following this clear track past a couple of houses on the right. Go through a gate and continue on the track until it meets a farm drive (Plas-bychan). Turn right along the drive and continue over a cattle grid, now walking on a surfaced lane. Pass a drive to farm buildings on the right and continue along the lane as it bears left down to the road (approx 800m from the first farm to the road). Turn right and walk along the road all the way back to the village (over 2km) to complete the walk.

The imposing cream building on the hillside to the left, before you reach the village, is Garthewin, which was the family seat of the Wynne family for over three centuries until it was finally sold in 1996.

Moel Unben

Cyffylliog

Distance: *8km/5 miles*

A delightful walk from this unspoilt village that nestles amongst the tree clad hills of the Clwyedog valley. The walk leads along the upper reaches of the Clwyedog and then along quiet lanes with wide views out to sea. The return is made on an old track across farmland with views of the forested hills.

Start: There is limited roadside parking in Cyffylliog. *Grid ref: 060 578 (OS Explorer map 264).*

Cyffylliog has a peaceful air, hidden away in the valley bottom. The simple terraced cottages, the inn and village school, with its distinctive bell tower, are attractive, but it is the setting, high in the wooded Clywedog valley, threaded by narrow wildflower-edged lanes that gives its special quality.

The walk

1. This circuit partly follows one of the waymarked walks in the Mynydd Hiraethog and Denbigh Moors footpath network developed by Conwy and Denbighshire Councils. Look for 'Mynydd Hiraethog' green circular waymarker discs.

From the bridge walk towards the Red Lion pub and take the lane on the right signed to 'Nantglyn'. Walk along the lane passing the church on the right.

Cyffylliog church is small with a simple stone belltower, set in a pretty churchyard with old gnarled yews. Next to the churchyard is a Georgian 'hearse house', a small stone building with large wooden doors, built to house the horse-drawn hearse.

Just past the church, take the waymarked footpath on the right immediately before a cottage. Follow the path over the river by a footbridge and bear left, walking with the river on your left.

The path leads to an old fording point on the river. Turn right along the waymarked riverside path, ignoring a bridge on the left. Follow this path through woodland with the river close by for approximately 1km / ¾ mile as it climbs gradually.

The Clywedog is fast flowing here, running over large slabs of stone and forming small waterfalls. An attractive mix of trees, including wild cherry and hazel grow on the steep banks which are carpeted with wild garlic in spring.

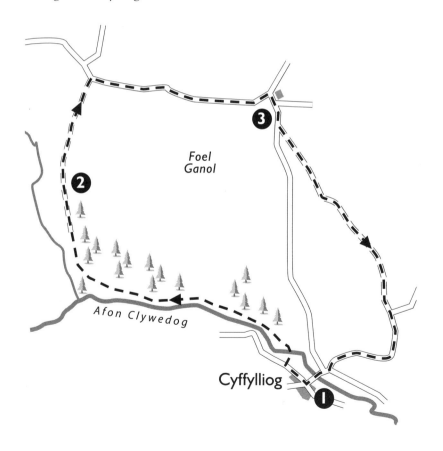

As you leave the woods, a gate leads onto an access track that curves right to a cottage out of view up to the right. Go ahead along the access track and where it begins to drop to cross a bridge bear right on a narrow woodland footpath.

This path leads along the right-hand side of the river and widens as it climbs up the hillside, with conifers on the right and a steep drop down to the river on the left. Continue on the path as it bears right away from the river. At the first path junction bear left downwards to a T junction. Turn right here and continue uphill on a good forest track.

2. Cross a gate or stile at the edge of the forestry plantation and follow the rising track, leaving the Hiraethog Trail, and climbing up away from the river. Continue uphill to a lane. Turn right onto the lane, rejoining the Hiraethog Trail, and continue for about 1.5km.

Rising out of the Clywedog valley with views to the Denbigh Moors

Turn right and continue along the lane for about 1.5 km/1 mile.

There are wide views to the left stretching out to the distant coast. In the foreground is the green rolling farmland of the Vale of Clwyd with the tower of Llanrhaeadr church just visible on a clear day and the northern Clywdians beyond. As you walk along the lane, views of the Clwydians change, as first Moel Arthur and then Moel Famau appear.

3. At a fork in the road, bear right, passing stone farm buildings on the left. Ignore a signed footpath on the right and continue ahead for 100 metres over a cattle grid, then take a clearly waymarked footpath immediately on the left. Follow this very clear grassy track for approximately 1.5km/1 mile, gradually descending towards Cyffylliog.

The views are superb again with the Clocaenog Forest across the valley and rolling farmland with thick hedges and pockets of woodland all around.

At a gate and stile, cross over and continue ahead to the road. Turn right and walk along the road downhill. At the bottom of the hill turn right, cross the river on the main bridge and walk back into the village to complete the walk.

Clocaenog Forest

Distance: *9.5km/6 miles*

A refreshing walk through the hilly coniferous forest and along quiet lanes with some superb views.

NB—Please note that this is a working forest and felling operations may occasionally affect some of the paths.

Start: There is a small pull-in and limited roadside parking around the signed footpath to Pincyn Llys, 3.5km/2 miles west of Bontuchel. (From Bontuchel take the road signed Clocaenog and after 0.7 miles take the right turn towards Hiraethog). *Grid ref: 065 557 (OS Explorer map 264).*

The walk

1. From the pull-in take the path signed to 'Pincyn Llys' leading uphill through fairly open woodland with bilberry and heather. (The path is also marked with pink Mynydd Hiraethog waymarkers as some of this route overlaps with sections of the Mynydd Hiraethog linear footpath.) Cross a forest track and continue straight ahead on the waymarked path uphill towards a clearing. Continue to the large stone obelisk at the top of the hill.

This is the Lord Bagot Monument. The Bagots were important landowners in the area whose estate extended over 17,500 acres in the 18th and 19th centuries. The monument was erected by the second Lord Bagot in 1832 to commemorate the planting of the surrounding conifer plantations. They were felled during the First World War and the present forest was established in 1930s when the Forestry Commission began to replant the area.

There are fine panoramic views from the monument—the Arans beyond Bala can be seen to the southwest; the Berwyns to the southeast and the Clwydians to the east with the rolling Vale of Clwyd in the foreground and the lower wooded hills around Bontuchel to the north.

From the monument, facing back down the original path, walk forward a few metres, then turn left and follow a narrow grassy path, running west into the trees. Keep on this path through the plantations and felled areas (can be extremely boggy in felled area just before track junction). Keep going in same direction until you reach a junction where two wide forestry tracks merge. Continue ahead on the forestry track for about 750m until it meets the road. Turn left and walk along the road for just over 1km, ignoring the first forestry track on the left.

2. 300 m after 'Cefn Ddu' cottage on the right, turn left along a non-waymarked broad forestry track. Follow this track passing

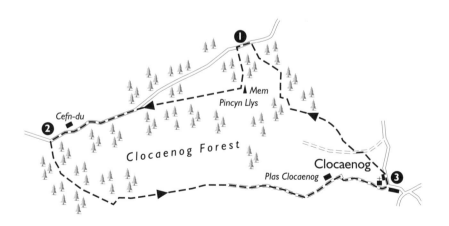

a very overgrown lake on the right (no open water was visible at time of checking) and ignore a track on the left opposite the lake.

Look for the white fluffy flower heads of bog cotton in the summer and the colourful dragonflies that breed in the acidic water. The dark green rushes and yellow and red sphagnum mosses indicate the boggy areas around the open water.

Where the path joins from the right, beside a fingerpost, continue ahead, once again on the 'Mynydd Hiraethog' waymarked route. At the next path junction take the waymarked track on the left. At a T junction in front of a gate into fields, turn

The Clocaenog Forest and Pincyn Llys

left and then bear right, following the waymarker. Continue on this path skirting the edge of the forest with farmland on the right.

At the next path junction beside a finger post, leave the main gated forestry track that curves left, and continue ahead on a smaller path leading downhill. At the next path junction, take the right-hand path that gradually leads away from the forest and has wide open views. Continue along this path as it descends to join a lane. Continue downhill on the lane, passing the attractive cluster of buildings at Plas Clocaenog farm on the right. Follow the lane to the village of Clocaenog.

The pretty church at Clocaenog, with its simple bellcote, stands on a hillock above the village. Its position may have given the village its name as 'Clocaenog' means 'grassy knoll'.

3. Pass the church and turn left at the road junction. At the edge of the village, cross a stile on the left and walk diagonally through the centre of the field to another stile in the bottom fenceline. Cross a boggy area beyond the stile, then over a small footbridge and climb steeply up the field to another stile. Cross onto a track and turn left. Walk along the track approximately 60m then take a narrow path on the right along the woodland edge. The path climbs steeply uphill with fields on the right and woods on the left. Cross a forestry track and continue ahead on a narrow path, still climbing. Where the path meets a broader track turn left and continue uphill for a few metres. At T junction of tracks at the top of the hill turn right onto a wide forest track.

There are now wide views of the Clwydian Range on the right.

Follow this track for about 1km as it contours round the hillside through more woodland, ignoring paths to left or right, until it reaches the road. Turn left and walk 70 m back to the pull-in by the Pincyn Llys sign to complete the walk.

Melin-y-Wig & Derwen

Distance: *12km/8 miles*

A longer but varied walk through forest, a quiet lane that was once a pilgrims' route and attractive riverside.

NB - The section through the forest south of Glan y Gors is very boggy. Waterproof boots are essential and it is rough underfoot. If you prefer you can avoid that section by just doing the loop from Derwen to Melin-y-Wig. (see map).

Start: Park at Boncyn Foel-Bach Forest Enterprise car park. There are picnic tables on the hillside here with wide views across the Vale of Clwyd. *Grid ref: 055 520 (OS Explorer map 264).*

(There are more facilities—toilets, and a pleasant lakeside walk—at the larger Forest Enterprise car park at Bod Petryal 2km further along the road but the footpaths don't easily link with this route.)

The walk

1. From the car park climb steps past picnic tables and walk uphill keeping a fence on the left and young trees on the right. At the corner of a field turn left onto a clear path along a beech avenue, alongside a field. At the end of the field just before a wooden seat turn right uphill onto a narrower path. Where this path joins a wider track turn left and continue, passing a pond on the left. At next track junction bear left and continue to downhill to a T junction of tracks. Turn left here and follow track to the road.

Cross the road and continue ahead down the access road to Glan y Gors, passing farm buildings on the right. Beyond the buildings go through a gate and cross the field to a stile in the opposite fence. Cross the stile and continue ahead across an area of young trees on a very faint overgrown path. Cross a wide forest track and continue straight ahead up the bank and along an overgrown path through conifers, keeping the remains of an old stone wall on the right. Continue along faint path through the mature conifers to a stile over the stone boundary wall on

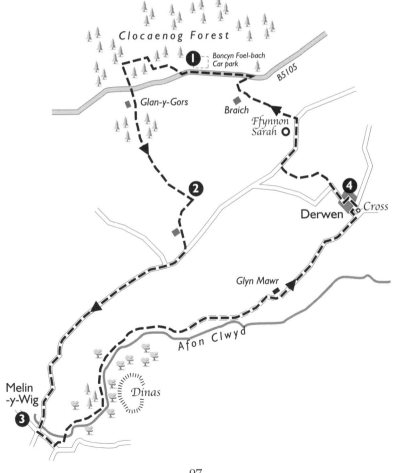

97

the far side of the forest. (NB: At time of writing the first section was very overgrown and the later section through the mature conifers was very boggy in places!) Climb the stile into fields and follow a sunken grassy path between old stone walls down the hillside.

The mound on the hillside to left is a Stone Age burial cairn. Lovely views open out here of the gorse capped, sheep grazed hills, dotted with twisted trees and with stone walls snaking up the hillsides. Buzzards are common, circling and crying overhead.

2. When you reach a farm drive turn right through a gate and follow the footpath to another farm on the right. Walk through the farmyard and along the farm drive to the lane, passing fishing lakes on the left. Turn right onto the lane and continue for 3km, finally walking downhill into Melin-y-Wig.

This quiet winding lane formed part of the medieval pilgrim track from St Winifred's Well at Holywell in the north-east corner of Wales, to the tomb of St David in Pembrokeshire at its south-western most tip.

Milling was obviously important here as 'Melin' means 'mill'. The old stone buildings on the right near the bridge over the river may once have been part of the mill complex.

3. At a road junction just beyond the bridge bear left and, after approximately 40m, turn left along a drive just beyond a chapel. Partway down the drive turn right over a stile and follow the path along the right-hand riverbank. Continue ahead when the path joins a grassy track leading in front of a cottage with the river on the left. Cross a footbridge over the river and turn right, following a narrow path along the left-hand bank of the river. Climb a stile and continue along this narrow natural path for approximately 1km across the base of a forested hillside with the river on the right.

The wooded hill on the opposite side of the river is crowned by an Iron Age hillfort ('Dinas' on the OS maps) but it is difficult to pick out the ramparts nowadays due to the thick tree cover.

Derwen church and medieval preaching cross

After a section of riverside walking follow the path along a fenceline as it bears left away from the river to a stile. Cross the stile and continue ahead across a grassy meadow beside the river. (NB—Can be wet!) Cross another stile and continue on path above the river to an old broken stile in the fence ahead. Cross this stile by the fence corner and continue ahead uphill for about 30m to meet a curving track. Turn right and follow the track back down to a meadow beside the river. Walk across the meadow (NB - Can be boggy!) and over a stile into the next field. Cross the field and go through a gate leading past an old cottage on the left. Continue along the drive of the cottage.

There are good views across the valley. The limestone quarry on the opposite hillside is one of several in the area, providing the mellow grey stone used in many of the local buildings.

After about 1km the drive bears left beside farm buildings (Glyn Mawr) and becomes a lane. Continue along the lane for about 1km, as it contours along the valley until you reach Derwen.

You may wish to detour into the churchyard of the medieval church to see the fine 15th century preaching cross in the churchyard. The church is no longer in regular use but is open to the public.

4. At the road junction opposite Derwen church, cross the road, then turn left and walk round the churchyard walls. Take the left turn at the end of a row of cottages opposite, signed Melin-y-Wig.

Follow this lane uphill to a small junction beside a chapel on the left. Take the tiny lane opposite which quickly deteriorates to become an overgrown track. Where the track narrows, after approximately 250m, go through a gate on the left and walk across a large field, aiming for tall trees on the skyline ahead. Go through a gate in the fenceline to the left of trees and then walk down the right-hand edge of the next field to a stile onto the road. (at time of writing the road verge beyond the stile was very overgrown). Turn right along the road and continue for

750m, passing 'Minffordd' cottage and Glan-y-aber farm track entrance, to the drive to Braich Farm on the left. Just before Braich Farm drive behind a stonewall and hedge on the left is 'Ffynnon Sarah', a medieval holy well. Detour through the gate onto a paved flat path that leads to where the spring bubbles into a tree shaded stone bath, now green with moss. The water was believed to have cured rheumatism and cancer. Pilgrims dropped in gifts of pins and those cured left their sticks and crutches as thanks offerings. It was still in use in Victorian times.

Turn immediately left up and walk up the long drive to Braich farm. Go through gates into farmyard and walk between a barn on the left and the farmhouse on the right. Then go through a gate into a small paddock on right behind farmhouse and through a second gate straight ahead into a larger field. Walk up the next field parallel to a stream on the right-hand side to a gate in the top corner. Go through the gate and bear right upwards on a muddy grassy track along the field edge climbing uphill. Go over the next stile and follow the grassy track diagonally up the field to a waymarker post and stile beside the road. Turn left onto the road and walk carefully back to the forestry car park to complete the walk.

Llangernyw

Distance: *6km/3¾ miles*

A delightful walk centred upon the pretty village of Llangernyw, leading along a terraced woodland path beside a cascading stream through the former 'pleasure gardens' of Hafodunos Hall. The return to the village is along peaceful lanes and beside the Afon Elwy.

Start: *Park near the public toilets (left down the lane beside the church) or car park beside the Henry Jones Museum (opposite the Bridge Inn). Grid ref: 876 674 (OS Outdoor Leisure map 17).*

Llangernyw is a very pretty village with its whitewashed church and old inn, set amongst rolling hills. St Digain's church has been a Christian place of worship since the 6th century but the 4,000 year old yew—the oldest in Wales—may indicate that it was originally a pagan site of worship as Christian churches were often sited on earlier pagan sites for continuity of worship.

The walk

1. From the church turn left along the main road towards Llanrwst. Turn right beside the Bridge Inn and follow the path alongside the pub to the riverside. (Muddy at the time of writing due to works going on by the river). Go through a kissing gate and walk across the field, keeping close to the river, to a small footbridge. Cross the river and walk along the path to the road. Turn left along the road and, approx 60m up the hill, turn left onto a footpath beside a dilapidated gatehouse, along the old drive of Hafodunos Hall.

'*Hafodunos*' — '*house of one night*' — *is a name more usually given to one of the tiny temporary homes of the herdsmen taking livestock up for summer grazing on the moors. At first one wonders how this name came to be given to such a grand house that obviously took years to complete. However, it was built on the site of a monastery and there may have been a rest house there for pilgrims — hence 'house of one night'.*

About 60m along the drive turn left onto a waymarked footpath into woods. This section along the river is very clearly waymarked and well maintained with steps and handrails so the route directions are not detailed. Bear right down steps towards the river. Continue along this delightful path, eventually zigzagging uphill away from the river.

This section of the walk leads through what was once part of the pleasure gardens of the house and it is was planted luxuriantly with

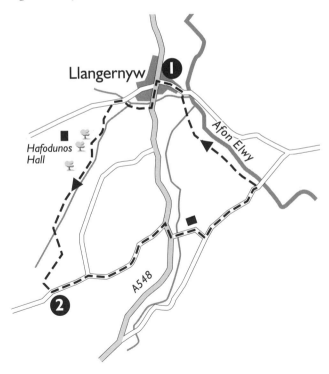

exotic species — the rhododendrons on the banks and clumps of bamboo nearer the river are the most obvious that remain. These blend well with the natural woodland that clothes the opposite bank, with the fast flowing river below, cutting through stone, with small waterfalls as it tumbles down the hillside. Damp loving plants like golden saxifrage, a small yellowish green plant with rounded leaves, ferns and mosses abound. Pale green feathery lichens hang down from the trees. They only grow in areas that are pollution free, so their abundance here indicates how clean the air is.

Follow the woodland path (still waymarked) to a ladder stile on the woodland edge. Cross the stile and continue ahead. Go through a small gate and continue ahead, skirting woodland on the right, with the river on the left. Cross a footbridge over the

The memorial to the Sandbach family

stream and walk up stone steps, then along the field edge. Climb another ladder stile and bear slightly left (following direction of waymarker) across this large field to a hedge on the far side (about 300 m). Turn right at the field boundary (near a waymarker by a gate) and continue along the left-hand field edge to a gate in the far left corner. Beyond the gate, follow the path to the road.

2. Turn left along the road and, when you reach a junction with a grassy triangle in the centre, bear right along a narrow lane. Pass several buildings and continue along the lane which becomes more overgrown and track-like. When the track joins a road, turn right and, after 120m, turn left at the next junction, signed 'Gwytherin'.

Follow this lane past farm buildings and bear left at the first road junction. Continue to a T junction and turn left. Follow this quiet road to a bridge over the river. Turn left onto a footpath just before the bridge. Meander through the field and grassy clearing keeping the river on your right, then cross a stile concealed in the far left-hand corner of the field and climb uphill on an overgrown grassy path with the river down on the right. Cross two more stiles into a large field (ignore a waymarker to the left) and continue walking ahead beside the river. At the next field boundary, cross a stile and walk across the field, keeping the river on the right, to a small footbridge in the middle of the field. Cross the bridge, turn right and follow the left-hand hedgerow to a smaller footbridge. Continue to a stile onto the road by a stone bridge. Turn left along the road to return to the village to complete the walk, detouring through the churchyard on the left if preferred.

The large stone mausoleum stands out amongst the gravestones in the churchyard. It bears testament to the wealth and influence of the Sandbach family—Samuel Sandbach, a Liverpool merchant and shipowner, bought nearby Hafodunos Hall in 1831 and several generations of the family have left their mark on the village.

Llansannan

Distance: *12km/8 miles*

A longer but varied walk alongside the River Aled and its tributaries, through rolling pasture edged with thick hedgerows and pockets of woodland, with a backdrop of mountains.

This circuit follows sections of a series of waymarked walks developed by Conway County Borough Council. For further information on the complete booklet, 'Walks around Rural Conwy', contact the council on: 01492 575200.

Start: *Park in the car park opposite the Post Office, behind the public toilets in Llansannan village.*
Grid ref: 933 658 (OS Explorer map 264).

The walk

1. From the car park turn right and walk to the road junction opposite the Red Lion. Turn left and walk along the road, past the Saracen's Head pub. Just after the road crosses the river, take the footpath signed on the left, opposite a white house 'Y Llety', along a clear track. Cross a cattle grid and gate and continue along the track which gradually descends to the riverside.

The wide fast flowing river is edged with trees—particularly alder that thrive in the damp conditions. Look for dippers—small brown birds with white breasts that bob across the rocks—and grey wagtails—slender grey birds with long tails and yellow undersides. Both are commonly seen, feeding on insects, on the rocky rivers and streams in the area.

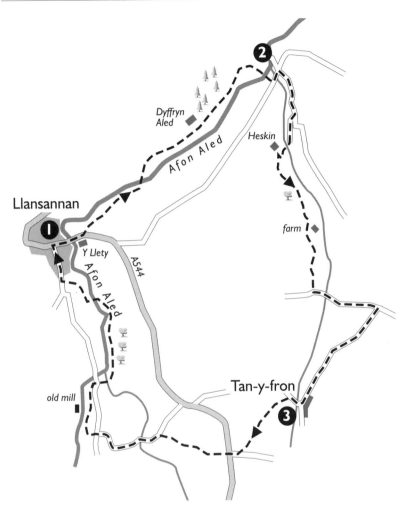

At a T junction of tracks, turn left over a bridge and continue along the track over another cattle grid, ignoring a path signed off to the left. Pass a house on the right and continue on the rising track. Further on ignore a track off to the left.

Just before a house (Dyffryn Aled), bear right off the drive into a field then curve left to walk along the left-hand field edge, passing the house on the left. Just beyond the house cross a stile

Looking towards Mynydd Tryfan

on the left and continue ahead through 'ornamental' grounds to join a woodland track. Continue on the woodland track going straight ahead at a path junction. At the end of the woodland, continue on the track beside a pasture. Cross a stile and walk along path that soon becomes a track to cross a bridge over the river (Afon Aled).

2. Follow the track to the road. Turn left and walk downhill to a crossroads. Turn right here, signed to 'Capel Horeb' and 'Tan-y-Fron'. Follow the lane for 500m, passing 'The Old Mill' and walking beside the stream.

(If you want a more strenuous walk and are equipped with a detailed map, you may wish to detour up a footpath on the left into woodland, soon after 'The Old Mill' on right. This leads up Mynydd Tryfan which has wide views from the top. There is a clear track back down from Arllwyd farm which can link back to the road at Tan Tryfan, grid ref: 966 655.)

Where the lane starts to climb steeply, turn right onto a lane signed 'no through road'. In about 250m, just before buildings, turn right down a concrete farm drive (unmarked in August 2008). Follow the drive initially downhill and over a stream and then uphill. Where the drive bends right to the farm, cross a stile on the left (straight ahead as you approach). Walk straight ahead across the field (ignore the other path signed to the right). Cross another stile and walk along the lower edge of the next field, passing a pond on the left, with the river below. Towards the end of the field, follow a waymarker down to the bottom left corner by the river. Climb a stile, cross the stream and another stile and climb up the opposite bank.

Walk diagonally-right steeply up the field heading for a waymarked gate part way along the far hedge. Go through the gate and continue ahead across a large field towards farm buildings. Keep metal barns on the left and go through a gate beside them into the farmyard. Turn right and follow the drive as it curves right past the farmhouse and outbuildings. Ignore a fork to the right, and continue along the long drive to the road. Turn left along the road, which climbs steeply for approximately 1km.

There are good views of Mynydd Tryfan on the left from this lane.

Where the gradient levels out, turn right on the lane signed to 'Tan-y-Fron' and follow it for approximately 1.5 km into the hamlet of Tan-y-fron. Ignore a lane on the left and continue downhill, signed Llansannan.

There are glimpses of the Snowdonian mountains to the left.

3. Follow the lane over the bridge in Tan-y-fron past a simple old chapel on the right with a house attached. About 60m uphill, take a footpath on left (the stile may be difficult to see in the hedgerow). Cross the field and climb another stile into the next field. Walk diagonally-right climbing steeply up the field, heading for a tall clump of trees by the fence. Cross a stile and walk diagonally-right across the next field towards farm buildings. Go

109

through a gate and turn left into the farmyard. Walk through the farmyard, passing the farmhouse on the right and walk along the farm drive to the road. Turn right at the road and walk to a T junction with more major road. Cross this road and climb up the bank opposite and cross a stile near a modern bungalow, Bryn Derw. Cross two more stiles linking small enclosures, then continue ahead, keeping the fence on the left. After passing a large pond on the left cross through the next gateway, then turn right and continue in the same direction as before with the fence now on the right.

Buzzards wheel overhead and you may hear their high pitched 'mewing' cry. Rabbits scurry for the safety of the undergrowth — startled by your approach but also rushing to avoid the buzzard, whose favourite food is rabbit!

At the end of the field, join a wider track and continue ahead through a gate. Walk along the left-hand edge of a large field. Where the field widens, continue ahead, bearing slightly right, to a stile in the far corner. Cross into a narrow field and walk downhill beside the right-hand fenceline. Partway down the field, cross a stile on the right onto the road. Turn left along the road and walk downhill, crossing a stream and passing a white cottage on the right, then continue uphill. At a road junction, cross over and continue ahead on a little lane passing a stone cottage, Bryn-hyfryd, on the right. Continue on the path down to the river (Afon Aled). Ignore the bridge on the left and continue ahead on a signed path along the right-hand bank of the river, passing the old mill on the left bank.

The river is fast flowing here, tumbling over rocks and making a small waterfall. The mill wheel is no longer in place but it is easy to see why it was such a good location for the mill — harnessing the torrent of water here must have generated lots of power.

Follow the path along the river to the road. Cross the road and take the path immediately opposite, beside the river. At a waymarker post bear right up a narrow path and then descend steeply into a field. Cross the field to a stile and footbridge opposite. Go over the bridge then turn left up the bank and walk beside the river along a faint grassy path that meanders through natural woodland. The path isn't always clear and crosses an area of bracken which may be tall in the summer but keep walking parallel to the river.

Where the path reaches a hedgerow cross a stile on the left just above the river and walk along the field edge, still keeping the river on the left. Continue across fields in the same direction beside the river to a footbridge. Cross the footbridge, and then walk straight across the field to an old stone wall and hedge opposite. Turn right and walk along the track towards farm buildings. Go through a gate into the farmyard and follow the farm drive to the road. Turn right and follow the road back into Llansannan. At a T junction in the middle of the village turn right past a shop and then left before the Saracen's Head to return to the car park and complete the walk.

The statue on the left beside the road junction in the village centre is the Llansannan Monument—a girl in a Welsh dress in front of an obelisk. It was erected in 1899 to commemorate five writers born in the area over the preceding centuries.

Gwytherin

Distance: *7km/4½ miles*

A refreshing walk centred on this pretty and peaceful village, up a wooded valley and across open moorland with wide views of Snowdonia.

NB—Some sections of this walk, across heather moorland, are extremely boggy. When visibility is poor, route finding across the moors may be a problem unless you have a map and compass, so save this walk for a dry clear day when the views of Snowdonia are spectacular and the moorland is alive with birdsong.

Start: *There is roadside parking in the village or large pub car park (ask the landlord's permission first).*
Grid ref: 877 615 (OS Outdoor Leisure map 17).

Gwytherin village centre is clustered around a small stone enclosed square containing an old anvil, edged by its simple church, pretty cottages and the Lion Inn. Legend has it that St Winifred, the martyred saint of Holywell, became an abbess of a convent here which is why Gwytherin church takes her name. In the attractive oval churchyard are four large stones that may date from the 6th century.

The walk

1. Opposite the church, take the footpath that runs alongside a stream to the right of the pub. Pass a cottage on the left and walk uphill along a narrow path, keeping the stream down on the left. Cross a stile and follow the waymarked path uphill. Gradually bear right away from woodland and the stream into a field then continue climbing in the same direction as before, passing a small outcrop on the right (NB - the path isn't very clear). Continue uphill, passing a small fenced field on the right in front of old farm buildings. Cross a stile by a waymarker in the fence ahead. Turn right and walk towards the stone farm buildings and sheep pens—this is the sheep gathering area of Pen-y-graig farm so please take care and keep dogs on leads. Bear left before the buildings, following waymarker on post, and walk behind the buildings. Beyond the buildings, cross a stile onto a track. Turn left and follow the track uphill.

Keep walking on this clear track, for about 800m, going through one gateway and ignoring the first path on the right by another gate. When you reach a fence ahead and the main path bears right through a gate, turn left onto the moorland and walk

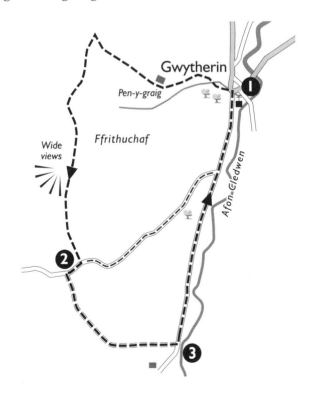

Looking northwest from Ffrithuchaf

alongside the fence. Continue walking across the moors, keeping the fence on the right. (NB - this section is extremely boggy!)

During the spring and summer the moor is filled with the haunting call of the curlew—a high pitched 'coorl-li' and you are likely to see some of these large waders with their long down-curved beaks as they take off at your approach. They spend winter on the coast and then fly inland to breed on the moors. Heather thrives in the drier areas—the delicate pale lilac flowered ling and bell heather with its larger bright pinkish-purple flowers. In the many wetter areas are dark green rushes, red tinged grasses and patches of green and red moss—much of it is sphagnum, the spongy moss that horticulturalists use to line their hanging baskets as it holds water so well.

Follow the fence as it turn sharply right and walk down to a fence junction with an old stile. Do not cross the stile but turn left and continue walking with the fence on your right. Ignore a stile and waymarker on the right soon after this and continue walking alongside the fence.

There are wide views of the Snowdonian peaks on a clear day. Moel Siabod is the bulky peak to the left followed by the Snowdon group, the Glyderau, Tryfan and rounded bulk of the Carneddau. The large turbines in the foreground are one of several windfarms being erected in Hiraethog to generate renewable energy.

Go through a gate and keep walking straight ahead, with the fence on the right until you reach a stile at the fence junction ahead. Cross the stile (broken when route was checked in March 09) and bear diagonally-left slightly uphill at first then downhill across a hummocky extremely boggy field. Cross a ditch and continue to a fence enclosing a brighter green field (ignore stiles in and out of this enclosure). Turn right and walk alongside this fence to a gate in the field corner ahead. Go through the gate and walk downhill across this field to go through a gate onto the road.

2. Turn right along the road, and after 200m turn left through first gate onto a grassy path that descends hillside through a rough field. Ignore a right fork that bends uphill and continue descending on the clear grassy track. Go through a gate and keep descending. Partway down the hill at another track junction (a muddy sheep feeding area in winter – keep dogs under control) swing left on the track steeply downhill, ignoring path up to a gate on the right. Continue on this lower path, over a stream then gradually descending, ignoring a path uphill on the left. Continue on the track with the stream down on the right.

The exact location of St Winefride's Abbey is uncertain but some think it was in this secluded valley and that the scattered stones and odd low wall down on the opposite side of the stream may be the remains of the abbey.

3. Go through gate into the farmyard and turn left past a barn and follow the farm drive down to road. Turn left and walk along road for 2km back into Gwytherin to complete the walk.

Llyn Brenig

Distance: *12km/8 miles or 5km/3 miles*

Enjoy the open water of Llyn Brenig, fringed with conifer forests and the wild Hiraethog moors.

Start: *Pay and display parking is available at Llyn Brenig Visitor Centre. Grid ref: 967 548 (OS Explorer map 264).*

Welsh Water, who manage the reservoirs, encourage visitors and have developed a variety of walks:- a surfaced, easy to follow 10° mile circular walk around the lake; a 2 mile archaelogical trail from the car park on the eastern side and a 7 mile waymarked trail around nearby Llyn Alwen A good starting point for a first visit is the visitor centre where the trail leaflets can be bought and there are informative displays. There is also an adventure playground and cafe so it makes an ideal family outing.

If you want a more varied walk, the one described here links a walk along the dam wall with a pleasant exploration of the Aled valley beyond the dam. The circuit from Pentre-llyn-cymer is one of a series of walks in Mynydd Hiraethog developed by Conwy and Denbighshire Councils. It is waymarked with 'Mynydd Hiraethog' green discs but, at time of rewriting, some of the discs were missing.

If you just want a very short circuit including the dam a shorter option is also described.

The walk

1. Park in the main Visitor Centre car park. Walk down to the reservoir edge past the Visitor Centre and turn right along the water's edge. Go through a small gate and follow this path alongside the reservoir to the dam. Turn left and walk along the wide track which tops the dam wall.

The high rainfall and low population on the moors made it an ideal site for a reservoir. The first scheme was proposed in the 1900s to provide water for Birkenhead. Construction of the Alwen reservoir was completed in 1916 but it was not until 1976 that Lyn Brenig was

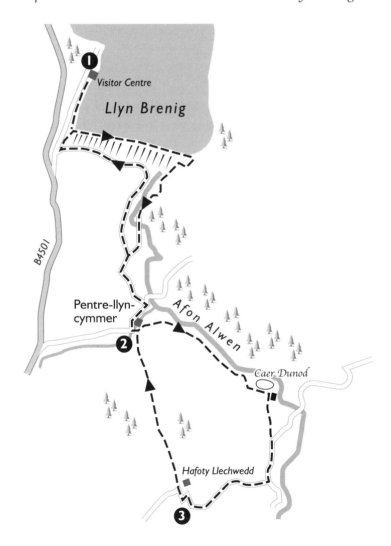

opened. *The reservoirs now provide water for industrial and domestic use in Chester and northeast Wales and are used to regulate the flow of water in the River Dee, preventing flooding in the winter and drought in the summer. The small tower in the water beside the dam regulates the flow of water from the reservoir.*

There are wide views from the dam across the moors and forested hilltops. 3,500 years ago Bronze Age tribesmen hunted on these moors and the area is dotted with their burial mounds. Many have been carefully excavated and several well preserved examples can be seen on the archaelogical trail to the northeast of the reservoir.

At the end of the dam take the track on the right that curves down behind the dam. After about 200m, turn left along a wide grassy track leading above a stream and weir in the valley below on the right. Cross a stile into the forest and, after about 30 metres, turn right and walk along a path at edge of trees. At the woodland edge go through a gate onto a lane with a static caravan park on the left. Continue on this lane over a bridge and uphill.

(If you want a short route, turn right onto a signed footpath partway up this lane. Walk diagonally-right across the field and strip of woodland to the road. Turn right onto a narrow road and follow this back below the dam to the left-hand (western) side of reservoir.)

Follow the lane to a road junction. Continue ahead along the road, bearing sharply left and downhill after 100m. Continue past farm buildings on the right to a T junction at the bottom of the hill. Turn right and walk along the road into the hamlet of Pentre-llyn-cymmer.

2. Turn left across a small bridge towards the Outdoor Centre and right along a track in front of this. Climb a stile by a gate, then immediate left over a second stile (not waymarked) and follow the path ahead, first skirting along the left-hand edge of a large field and then walking with the river below on the left. At the end of the field cross a stile by a Mynydd Hiraethog green waymarker and continue ahead across the next field, with

The dam, Llyn Brenig

the river below on the left. Continue across fields, gradually descending to walk alongside the river. Pass a cottage on the opposite bank and walk towards woodland ahead (NB can be muddy when grazed by cattle).

The river edge is full of colour in summer—pinkish-white valerian, cream meadowsweet, masses of buttercups, tall pale green reeds and darker green rushes.

Climb a stile into woodland and follow a meandering narrow path through damp ground alongside the river (NB can be muddy). At the end of the woodland turn right away from the river skirting around the right-hand side of a hill ahead.

This small hill, Caer Ddunod, was once fortified and, although ruined by 17th century, may have once been of considerable importance— some even claim it was the site of Caractacus' last stand against the Romans!

The Visitor Centre, Llyn Brenig

Go through a gate and follow a track into a farmyard. Turn right past the farmhouse and continue along the farm drive. Where the drive meets a lane turn right and walk downhill, past a whitewashed cottage on the left. Where the main lane bends left, turn right onto a side lane and continue on this lane for over 1km, climbing steeply uphill. Eventually the angle eases and the road bends sharply right.

3. At the next sharp left-hand bend, with a farm, 'Hafoty Llechwedd', on the right, take the signed path straight ahead, leading behind the buildings.

A 'hafoty' or 'hafod' was a small summer dwelling, built by the herdsmen who brought cattle to graze the moors in the summer. There were many of these simple one-roomed stone huts in the 16th and 17th centuries but they fell into disuse as sheep farming gradually took over — as sheep do not require milking, the shepherds didn't need to live with the flocks. Perhaps one of the older farm buildings here may have originally been a 'hafoty'?

Go through the gate or stile and walk along the top of the next field. Go through a gateway (no gate) then turn left over a stile and walk diagonally-left across a large field, heading towards the left-hand edge of conifers. Pass a 'pile of stones' in the middle of the field.

Cross a stile and walk along the right-hand field edge, beside conifers, crossing another stile and continuing as path widens to a track. Go through a gate at end of the woodland and walk a short distance ahead along the wide track.

The Alwen Reservoir and dam comes into view on the left. The dam is particularly attractive with its turreted, romantic-looking water tower — quite different from the utilitarian one built at Brenig in the 1970s, but serving the same purpose.

Leave the main track, just after another track joins from the right, and walk diagonally-right across rough grass to a stile in the bottom right corner of the field under small power lines. (Take care as, at time of writing, this wasn't waymarked and could easily be overlooked.) Continue downhill along the right-hand fenceline to cross a stile on the right and continue downhill along the left-hand fenceline, following waymarker, back down to the path in front of the Outdoor Centre.

Retrace your steps through Pentre-llyn-cymer, turning right along the road and left up the lane past the farm. Continue uphill and soon after the lane bears sharply right, bear left instead of turning right onto the narrow lane that you used earlier. Follow this lane back to the base of the dam and either go through gap by gate ahead and follow curving track back onto the dam or turn left and follow the lane below the dam back to the left-hand (western) side of the reservoir. Retrace your steps along reservoir edge back to the Visitor Centre to complete the walk.

Pentrefoelas

Distance: *8.5km/5¼ miles*

The historic riverside village of Pentrefoelas is an ideal starting point for walks with its cafes, pubs and public toilets. The route climbs slowly onto open moorland, giving superb views of Snowdonia then descends along quiet lanes and old tracks back to the village.

Start: Walkers are asked to use the large car park behind the 'Foelas Arms' but there is also car parking, public toilets, and a picnic area beside the river opposite the pub.
Grid ref: 872 516 (Landranger 116, Explorer OL18).

The walk

1. From the car park at the back of the 'Foelas Arms' walk turn left onto the road and after a few metres, take the footpath on the right through a kissing gate, between houses and into a field.

One of these fields behind the houses was the site of the large Pentrefoelas Eisteddfod that was held from 1919 until 1925. They drew thousands from across Wales and were second only to the National Eisteddfod in importance. It grew rapidly, attracting over 20,000 in its final year, but ended due to a lack of financial backing and the problems of dealing with such large crowds.

Walk up the left-hand side of the field, following the stonewall. Go through a kissing gate and continue along left-hand edge of next field and through a metal gate. Continue ahead across the field and through a gate into woodland. Follow the track between farm buildings then through a gate. Cross a farm track and continue on clear path through woodland, passing a pond on the left. At the woodland edge go through the gate ahead and continue in same direction across the field, following left-hand hedge. Go through a kissing gate onto a tarmac lane and turn right along lane, ignoring footpath on left. Continue along the lane to a cattle grid.

2. Take the track on the left immediately after cattle grid and continue uphill on this clear path through fields, keeping close to left-hand field boundary and going through three gates. Turn right after the third gate beside a finger post, with the Mynydd Hiraethog waymarker.

It is worth pausing in this area to take in the views over Snowdonia.

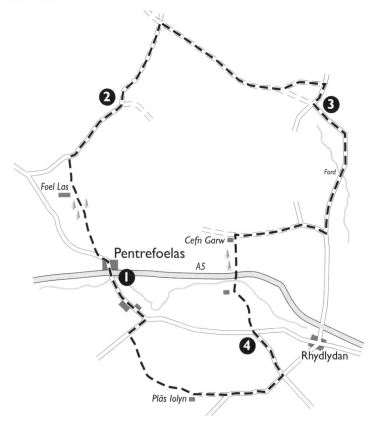

Looking towards the mountains of Snowdonia

Continue walking in same direction for just over 1km with stonewall/fence on the right and going through several gates. Go through another gate to continue down a sunken track with walls on both sides. Partway down the track turn left through a gate beside a waymarker post (propped up at time of writing!) and follow the clear path along the left-hand edge of fields. Go through a gate by a farm to join a lane then continue down the lane to the main road. Turn right along the main road (take care), walking downhill. After 250m turn left along a tarmac lane and follow this for approximately 750m.

3. Cross a cattle grid and then turn right onto a narrow lane and follow this downhill. Cross a stream via the ford or footbridge and continue uphill on this lane to a road junction. Turn right onto the wider road. Where this road bends right continue ahead on the track opposite (signed bridleway). Go through a gate, passing a cottage on the left, and follow the grassy track ahead with a stone wall on the left. Go through two gates and finally a third gate into the yard of 'Cefn Garw'. Turn left across the yard and through another gate into a field. Walk ahead downhill through fields, along the right-hand field edge, with woodland on the right. Carefully cross a stile at the bottom of the field onto the A5. Cross the road with great care (can be very busy) and take the path opposite down to a footbridge. Cross the bridge and walk up the field towards farm buildings. Turn right through a gate just before the farm then immediate left, passing the farmhouse on the left. Go through another gate and turn left at track junction, then follow the farm drive to the road.

4. At the road junction take the minor road opposite and follow this for about 500m to a cross roads. Turn right here and after about 600m bear right onto a drive, signed Plas Iolyn.

Plas Iolyn was formerly the home of the Price family, descendants of Rhys Mawr, standard bearer to Henry Tudor at the Battle of Bosworth. His son, Robert ap Rhys was a chaplain to Cardinal Wolsey and amassed a large estate. He built a mansion at Plas Iolyn. This was later rebuilt by his son Ellis Price who is better known as' y Doctor Coch' (the Red Doctor). According to legend, he combined a career in law with that of a highwayman, using the tower to spy out travellers on the old road to Ysbyty Ifan who were then attacked by his men.

Go past Plas Iolyn on left. Just beyond the out-buildings cross a ladder stile into a field and follow waymarked path down the right-hand edge of one field and the left-hand edge of the next, gradually descending. At farm buildings keep wall on left and go through a gate and over a stile to continue downhill to the road on the clear path. At the road turn right then left at the next junction and walk back into Pentrefoelas village. Cross A5 and continue on the minor road opposite, passing the Foelas Arms on the left, to return to the car park and complete the walk.

Pentrefoelas was an important staging point for drovers moving cattle from west Wales to market in England. Four annual fairs were held until the 1920s where cattle and sheep were sold and workers hired. The Foelas Estate still own most of the surrounding land and much of the village was built by the estate in local stone, including a corn mill and workshops.

Mara Books & Alyn Books
www.marabooks.co.uk or www.alynbooks.co.uk

North Wales
Walking in the Clwydian Range
ISBN 978 1 902512 14 3. A collection of 21 circular walks exploring the Clwydian Range Area of Outstanding Natural Beauty (AONB). Illustrated with maps and photographs in both colour and black and white.

Wat's Dyke Way Heritage Trail
ISBN 978 0 9559625 0 9. A 61 mile linear walk through the English counties of Cheshire and Shropshire and the North Wales border, following the course of the Dark Age earthwork (www.watsdykeway.org).

Circular Walks in the Conwy Valley
ISBN 978 9522409 7 6. Twenty of circular walks which explore the varied scenery of this beautiful valley from the Great Orme to Betws-y-Coed.

Walking in Snowdonia *Volume 1*
ISBN 978 1 902512 06 8. A series of circular walks exploring the beautiful and dramatic valleys in the northern half of the Snowdonia National Park.

Coastal Walks around Anglesey
ISBN 978 1 902512 20 4. A collection of 15 walks which explore the varied scenery of Anglesey's beautiful coastline.

Walking the Isle of Anglesey Coastal Path
ISBN 978 1 902512 13 6. The official guide for the Isle of Anglesey Coastal Path. Full colour in English and Welsh.

Walking on the Lleyn Peninsula
ISBN 978 1 902512 00 6. A collection of 16 circular walks which explore the wild and beautiful coastline and hills of the Lleyn Peninsula.

A Pocket guide to Snowdon
ISBN 978 1 902512 16 7. A guide to all Snowdon's recognised routes of ascent, from the six 'Classic Paths' to the many lesser known and less frequented routes.

Snowdonia's best Mountain Walks
ISBN 978 1 902512 19 8. This book gathers the very best mountain walks to be enjoyed throughout Snowdonia.

Mountain & Hill Walking in Snowdonia
This is a two-volume in-depth guide to every summit of note in the Snowdonia National Park.

Volume 1 covers the Carneddau, Glyderau, Snowdon and Eifionydd ISBN 978 1 902512 18 1

Volume 2 the Moelwynion, Rhinogydd, Arenig, Arans, Dyfi hills and Cadair Idris as well as the Tarrens and berwyns ISBN 978 1 902512 22 8

Cheshire

Circular Walks along the Sandstone Trail
ISBN 978 1 902512 21 1. The Sandstone Trail is Cheshire's best known and most popular walking route. This book gives a complete route description along with 13 circular walks covering the entire trail.

A Walker's Guide to the Wirral Shore Way
ISBN 978 1 902512 05 1. A linear walk of 23 miles following the old coastline between Chester and Hoylake.

Circular Walks in Wirral
ISBN 978 1 902512 02 0. A collection of circular walks in the coast and countryside of Wirral.

Short Walks from Wirral Villages
ISBN 978 1 902512 23 5. A collection of 30 circular walks centered on Wirral villages. Ideal for families or those who don't want to walk too far.

Published by North Eye Books
www.northerneyebooks.co.uk

Walks in Mysterious Cheshire and Wirral
ISBN 978 0 9553557 0 7. A collection of 14 circular walks exploring Cheshire's historic landscape.

Walks in West Cheshire and Wirral
ISBN 978 0 9553557 2 1. Thirty of the best walks in west Cheshire and Wirral.

Walking Cheshire's Sandstone Trail
ISBN 978 0 9553557 1 4. The official guide to Cheshire's premier walking route. The trail is described in both directions and is complemented by full colour photographs and Ordnance Survey mapping.

Best Walks in North Wales
ISBN 978 0 9553557 3 8. A colection of 28 circular walks ranged throughout North Wales, from the wilds of the Lleyn Peninsula through Anglesey and Snowdonia to the rolling hills of the Clwydian Range.

Liverpool to Loggerheads
ISBN 978-0-9559625-2-3. This book celebrates the strong link between Merseyside and the Loggerheads area and is based on countless personal memories. It is lavishly illustrated with old photographs.